Television Today

PETER DOUGLAS

OSPREY

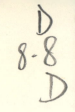

First published in 1975 by
Osprey Publishing Limited, 12–14 Long Acre,
London WC2E 9LP
Member Company of the George Philip Group
© Copyright 1975 Peter Douglas

ISBN 0 85045 067 5

Printed in Great Britain by
The Camelot Press Ltd, Southampton

Contents

1. The Historical Context

The history of radio in Britain

Because television is such an all-pervading influence in our lives we tend to forget that it is a comparatively late pheno-menon. Today's teenagers and those in their early twenties now are in fact only the first generation to have lived with television all their lives. And for those of us in our thirties, forties and over, radio – or the wireless, as we probably called it in those days – was still a source of wonder and entertainment during our childhood.

Yet the radio industry has been with us for not much over fifty years. Radio communication began a century ago. Experi-ments were carried out in 1864 by James Maxwell, a Scotsman, and in 1880 by Heinrich Hertz in Germany. Fifteen years later Guglielmo Marconi transmitted radio signals and in 1901 managed to broadcast across the Atlantic. In 1907 the vacuum tube – or valve as it came to be known – was patented by Lee de Forest and within a further five years the American navy were using broadcast signals for ship-to-ship communication.

The First World War put a halt to the progress of radio as an entertainment medium both in Britain and America, and it was not until 1921 that the first two radio stations, as we know them today, received licences to broadcast – at Pittsburgh, and Springfield, Massachusetts. A year later experiments using telephone lines to carry networked programmes proved successful and in 1927 America had its first coast-to-coast link-up. Round-the-world broadcasting first occurred in 1930 from Schenectady, USA.

The history of radio and television during the early years in Britain is inevitably bound up with the history of the British Broadcasting Corporation. Yet this great institution had its foundations firmly laid by some extremely commercial

1

interests, among them the manufacturers of radio equipment.

As early as 1919, just after the First World War, the Marconi Company had been licensed by the Post Office to carry out experimental broadcasts. A year later, with financial co-operation from the *Daily Mail*, they broadcast a concert given by Miss Nellie Melba. Such a frivolous use of the airwaves as it was then considered to be, led to a shutdown of all broad-casting for a year until powerful pressure groups forced the Post Office to grant another licence to the newly formed British Broadcasting Company in 1922. The company was made up of a consortium of equipment manufacturers, and the general manager they appointed was a Mr J. C. W. Reith.

By the end of the year, the Company was broadcasting up to five hours a day from London, with regional services operating in Birmingham and Manchester. Some rival radio stations still persisted, notably station 2-LO which broadcast from a rooftop in the Strand, close to the Company's own headquarters in Savoy Hill, for about an hour a day. Thanks largely to the comparatively small area of the British Isles, and to the excel-lent telephone trunk networks, by 1925 the Company could proudly claim that forty million people were within listening range of their broadcasts. About a million licences were issued, but there were probably five times the number of sets.

The reason for this is that the licence fee included a payment to the manufacturers of radio equipment in the form of a royalty, and this led to a boom in the sale of do-it-yourself home construction kits. Especially popular with youngsters of the day were primitive crystal sets that provided adequate listening.

Receivers were sold with two pairs of earphones, and an aerial made of a hundred feet of copper wire was recommended for good reception, and this had to be strung down the back garden on a long pole and correctly earthed against lightning. Receivers were not yet mains-powered but relied on wet accumulators which had to be taken to the local garage for recharging for a few pence. The licence fee was ten shillings (50p).

The pattern of programmes produced in the twenties was not a lot different from the one that persisted for forty years until the changeover to Radios 1, 2, 3 and 4, and in looking back over the history of both radio and television what is surprising is not the progress made forward, but the lack of it. Programmes consisted of concerts and dance band music, broadcast from the luxury hotels in central London. Bandleaders became household names and the new industry gave birth to the profession of song plugger – recruited from the publishing houses – and the first whiffs of payola. The bands were not paid for their broadcasts (the BBC felt the publicity given them was sufficient reward) and so were open to bribes from music publishers. The BBC hit back by not allowing the titles of tunes to be announced by the master of ceremonies. The bandleaders promptly got round this by introducing request spots that were rigged. The twenties also saw the first of the signature tunes that came to be associated with particular bands and celebrities, in much the same way that David Frost's television theme music became associated with him some fifty years later.

Radio plays were recorded live, often using several studios to obtain different sound effects. *Children's Hour* was also born at this time and tended to sound like a middle-class office party: the BBC staff did indeed leave their offices and went into the studio for the programme, playing the roles of uncle and auntie. There was also a steady diet of radio news and the first outside broadcasts.

Under Reith, the BBC took its duties seriously. Sundays, for example consisted of a diet of religion and serious music, with an early closedown, and these attitudes still prevail in television in the seventies with the Sunday evening 'God slot'. By January 1927, the Company was reorganized and the first Charter granted to the new British Broadcasting Corporation, as it became known, and this instrument has been renewed periodically ever since: in 1937, 1947, 1952, 1964, 1969 and in 1973. In March 1973, the Tory Government decided to extend the existing Charter by an additional five years, taking it until 1981, and pronounced that any further serious enquiry into the state of broadcasting was not called for at that time. A Labour Government came into power the following February and one of its first moves was to set in motion once again the enquiry into broadcasting, headed by Lord Annan, that it had tried to introduce during its previous administration. As we trace the history of radio and television in Britain, we shall see that two of its most pernicious developments – commercial television and, later, commercial radio – were sponsored by Conservative politicians.

By 1930 and in spite of Reith, a slightly less sober attitude reigned inside the BBC. Listeners were able to tune into the first of the vaudeville (variety) programmes and the equivalent of the present-day magazine programmes, in the form of *In Town Tonight*. This was a mixture of news, chat and music, which is very much the staple fare of Thames Television's *Today* programme or BBC's *Nationwide*. The year 1932 witnessed the move from Savoy Hill to a purpose-built complex at Broadcasting House, Langham Place, and the start of the Empire (later World) Service, from Bush House, Strand.

A year later, a primitive form of tape recording was discovered which was to revolutionize programming in the way that videotape affected television some decades later. Previously 'recording' had meant actually cutting a wax disc inside a cumbersome outside broadcast van.

In 1938, Reith resigned, feeling that his task was completed, and he took up the chairmanship of what was then Imperial Airways. A year later Britain was plunged into the Second World War.

The war was good for broadcasting. The country as a whole was united and radio programmes were designed to keep those at home cheerful. The Forces Programme, initiated in 1940, did a similar job for the troops abroad. The war years witnessed the start of the comedy shows such as *ITMA* (i.e. *It's That Man Again*) with comedian Tommy Handley. Vera Lynn was launched as the forces' sweetheart and request programmes such as *Housewive's Choice* and *Desert Island Discs* spawned the first disc jockeys in the shapes of Sam Costa, Jack Jackson and the young David Jacobs.

Older readers will recall the round-Britain and round-the-world link-ups, which reached their apotheosis in the tear-jerking two or three hours on Christmas afternoon before the King's message to his subjects. The war also led to the personalizing of news readers, the argument being that in the event of an invasion of Britain listeners would recognize the voice of the authentic news service. Meanwhile the Germans were beaming propaganda at Britain through the mouthpiece of Lord Haw-Haw.

The end of hostilities in 1945 saw the re-establishment of the Home and Regional Services – there had been only one channel during the war years. The Forces Programme became the 'Light' Programme and the Third Programme was introduced as the serious broadcasting channel. The immediate post-war years saw a fantastic rise in listenership: television, as we shall see in a moment, was still virtually unheard of. Radio serials such as *Mrs Dale's Diary*, *The Archers* and *Dick Barton, Special Agent*, could regularly draw audiences of fifteen to twenty million people. It was also the era of the great comedy variety shows – *Much Binding in the Marsh*, *Take It From Here* and of comedians like Tony Hancock.

Television arrived in 1952 but it was probably not until ten years later, in the early 1960s, that radio broadcasters really woke up to the fact. This is partly because right up to this time radio programmes such as *The Goon Show*, *Life with the Lyons*, *Beyond our Ken* and *Round the Horn* were still attracting healthy listening figures, especially on Sunday afternoons (where television still dies a death).

The major shake-up in radio came in 1964, when the old distinctions of Home, Light and Third Programmes were scrapped and replaced with Radios 1, 2, 3 and 4. Three of them are currently broadcast on both medium and long waves, and VHF; and most Radio 3 programmes and part of Radio 2's output are broadcast in stereo. Coverage of the entire British Isles was completed by the end of 1974. Schools broadcasts are allocated to Radio 4, and adult education to Radio 3, on medium wave. The Open University uses up to thirty hours a week on Radios 3 and 4, on VHF.

Ostensibly the four channels are designed to provide different and complementary types of broadcasting. Popular music (the BBC's description) is consigned to Radios 1 and 2, the former being more inclined towards pop, the latter to middle of the road and light music. Together these two channels account for some 80 per cent of all radio listening.

Radio 3 concerns itself with serious music of which about a hundred hours are broadcast weekly. There is some speech content of about eight hours a week, which includes drama, poetry, information and cultural programmes. Radio 4 is the major speech channel, including news and current affairs.

News bulletins are broadcast hourly between 7.00 am and 7.00 pm, and in between can be heard a mixture of plays, panel programmes, and some music. Features such as *Woman's Hour* and *You and Yours* (dealing with social problems) appear on this channel, as do major political and comment programmes which have a flavour of the old Third Programme.

BBC radio is also *regional* and there are Network Production Centres at Bristol (noted for its accent on natural history), Birmingham (where drama is a speciality) and Manchester. There are also studios in Newcastle, Leeds, Norwich, Plymouth and Southampton. Additionally there are regional centres in Northern Ireland (headquarters in Belfast with another radio studio in Londonderry); and Scotland (based in Glasgow, with area offices in Edinburgh and Aberdeen, and studios in Inverness and Dundee); and in Wales (based in Llandaff, with a studio at Bangor in the north).

There is also an entire BBC division labelled External Services, which broadcasts some 750 hours of radio a week, in forty languages. The programmes originate from Bush House, Strand, and are broadcast from transmitters in the United Kingdom (46 of them) and thirty relay stations dotted around the world. In addition External Services produce taped material for overseas consumption and each week some 300 tapes are despatched to seventy subscribing radio stations. These Topical Tapes, as they are called, are used by 250 stations in over fifty countries – including a hundred stations inside the USA.

This huge volume of radio output represents a considerable challenge to television in the seventies. But as if this was not enough, we have finally to look at *local* radio, both BBC and independent, in order to complete the picture of radio broadcasting in this country.

Radio in the United Kingdom started virtually on a localized basis and by 1924 there were already twenty low power stations operating, and at the time this was felt to be the only way in which the industry could expand. But with the development of high powered transmitters capable of reaching over wider areas, the local service was gradually condensed into the national service, supplemented by the activities of the regions described above.

By 1966, however, the concept of local radio was being re-

6

vived and the Government authorized the BBC to operate nine local stations, initially for a period of two years, on an experimental basis and broadly financed by the local authorities.

The first station to be so set up was at Leicester, in November 1967, and this was followed by others at Sheffield, Liverpool, Nottingham, Stoke-on-Trent, Brighton, Leeds and Durham. The experiment was considered a success but it was eventually decided that any further expansion would have to be financed out of an increased licence fee. The BBC was then duly authorized to establish up to forty local stations and proceeded to set up another twelve almost immediately. These were: Blackburn, Birmingham, Bristol, Derby, Humberside, London, Manchester, Medway, Newcastle, Oxford, Solent and Teesside, bringing the grand total to twenty.

A general election meanwhile brought the Conservatives to power in 1970. They were pledged to introduce local commercial radio and in March 1971 a White Paper was published confirming the existence of the twenty BBC stations but preventing any further development. In 1973, the Independent Broadcasting Act, which incorporated the Sound Broadcasting Act of the previous year, established the legal framework for setting up local 'independent' radio stations under the aegis of the Independent Broadcasting Authority (formerly the Independent Television Authority).

Unlike the central service of the BBC, the IBA does not produce programmes (either radio or television) but invites applications from programme contractors who set up the local stations, renting the IBA controlled transmitters and subject to the Authority's directives on output and advertising standards. The eventual target is a total of sixty stations, of which the first twenty-seven will reach half the population of Britain. The first seven, including the two London stations Capital and LBC, will reach $16\frac{1}{2}$ million people, or 30 per cent of the country's population. Programmes are to be transmitted on both medium waves (MF-AM) and VHF-FM.

The programme got under way with the establishment of the two London stations in the autumn of 1973. The two stations are designed to complement one another, Capital providing pop and light fare, while London Broadcasting is a news and

7

talk station – a formula that got both stations off to an extremely shaky start. LBC, through its news subsidiary, IRN, will eventually supply news to the other commercial stations, providing a service similar to that of the Independent Television News, which we will examine later.

Stations in Birmingham, Glasgow and Manchester opened in the Spring of 1974, and Tyneside and Swansea followed in the summer.

By the spring of 1975, Radio Hallam was operating in the Sheffield/Rotherham area, and Radio City in Liverpool. And stations were opening in Edinburgh, Plymouth, Nottingham and Teesside.

The unstable economic climate during 1974–75 and the change of government to Labour both cast clouds over the future of commercial radio in Britain. Some new stations are still planned at Bradford, Portsmouth, Ipswich, Wolverhampton, Belfast and Reading, but the prime areas are now exhausted and it will be increasingly difficult to attract bidders for any remaining franchises, when finance is necessarily related to advertising revenue.

The two London stations were distinguished by their internal disputes, sackings, resignations and cutbacks in service, and the regular listener quickly got the impression when tuning to LBC that the phone-in formula was being overworked, with the same uninteresting Cockney voices airing their personal grievances several nights a week. Certainly independent radio has not fulfilled the aspirations of its creators and further development is likely to be decelerated by the operation of market forces if nothing else.

Against the sketch I have just given of the background of radio broadcasting in Britain, we will proceed to look at the history of television. One question should be asked, however, even at this early juncture, and that is just how far broadcasting entertainment and information services can be extended until saturation point is reached? Independent radio stations, like commercial television, rely on advertising support for survival and it is arguable just how much advertising expenditure there is to go round. The proliferation of media must mean that other carriers of advertising (newspapers, magazines, etc.) must surely suffer. The scarcity of available revenue certainly provided serious problems for London Broadcasting in its early days, as advertisers chose the more popular Capital radio on which to peddle their wares. It is also questionable whether the public really needs this quite considerable range of choice. It is truer in broadcasting, than perhaps anywhere else, that more is not necessarily better, as any visitor to the United States will tell you. In spite of the six thousand local radio stations there and up to fifteen channels of television in the major cities there is still only limited choice: largely because all the alternatives are so bad.

Finally, in addition to the scarcity of listeners and cash available, there is the problem of the availability of talent. The expansion of broadcasting media does not automatically increase the amount of talent available, and if there is no money, the best cannot be bought. Inevitably, this must lead to a lowering of standards, simply as a result of trying to fill all the air time. The obvious example of this state of affairs again is sadly the experience in America, where anyone of even minimal intelligence shuns both television and radio and turns increasingly to old-fashioned books and newspapers.

The history of television in Britain

Let us now look at the development of television in the United Kingdom. Although television did not become a powerful entertainment force until the 1950s, early experiments with pictures by radio were being conducted at virtually the same time as wireless was in its infancy.

The inventor of the first television system was John Baird, who successfully demonstrated his system to the Royal Institution in January 1926. Two years later the BBC was asked by the Post Office to conduct further experiments, but the BBC were not satisfied with Baird's standards and turned to an alternative system being developed by Electrical and Musical Industries (Ltd). By 1933 further progress had been made, and three years later in 1936, the first television service in the world was put out by the BBC, using the Baird and EMI systems on alternate weeks. At the end of the year, the Baird system was scrapped.

Howard Bridgewater, who was chief engineer for BBC-TV from 1962 to 1968, recalls the early days: 'I worked with Baird for four years until 1932 and for the last two to three years of that period we had started some experimental broadcasts from a little studio. Just head and shoulders views of people each day, very simple things, but fascinating for the experimenters who in those days even made their own sets, adapted from radio sets.' (Quoted in *The New Priesthood* by Joan Bakewell and Nicholas Garnham – see Bibliography for details.)

Early problems at the BBC's Alexandra Palace studios included primitive cameras that could only work in extremely bright lighting, and early experiments with vision mixing devices, enabling the controller to exploit the possibilities of several cameras in one studio and change from one to the other. Even the earliest EMI system was using the 405 line standard in the early thirties (against Baird's 240 lines which caused flickering and some lack of definition).

By 1937 two studios were in operation and the BBC did its first outside broadcast – of the Coronation of King George VI. A short wave transmitter bounced the signal back to Alexandra Palace and this system meant that outside broadcasts had to work within a radius of some thirty miles from the Alexandra Palace mast. But they included Wimbledon and racing from Epsom, and ballet and plays from the West End of London.

It is estimated that there were about 20,000 viewers at this time and at the 1938 Radiolympia exhibition over twenty firms demonstrated a variety of domestic television receivers. These ranged from table models with a three-and-a-half-inch screen to larger cabinet models, mounted in expensive mock Chippendale and Adam surrounds.

The range of programmes was increasing all the time, with over a hundred plays a year (that is, two a week for the first three years!), with actors of the calibre of Laurence Olivier and Michael Redgrave. The service was all set to catch the public's imagination when war was declared on 3 September 1939.

While radio, as we have seen, made considerable strides during the war, even allowing for the restriction on channels, television, on the other hand, disappeared completely and without trace.

The service reopened in 1946 and the first programme was an outside broadcast of the June Victory Parade, preceded by a Mickey Mouse cartoon. The manufacture of sets had been halted almost completely during the war and many of those who viewed in 1946 were doing so on sets purchased some ten years previously. Then a fuel crisis and an unexpected cold snap forced the Government to close down the television service for a month – an experience that viewers of the January 1974 early closedown might regard with a somewhat wry humour.

Although the service quickly reopened, television was not without its problems, both artistic and technical. Many artists and their agents were frightened by television and would not allow performers to appear, and actors themselves worried about drying-up in front of the cameras: telerecording on videotape came later. However, the BBC managed to create the first of the major television personalities – Philip Harben, who gave cookery demonstrations, and Eamonn Andrews, who compèred *What's my Line?* were only two of them.

The technical problems included the very size and awkwardness of the equipment and the necessity for extremely powerful studio lighting which made even the most stalwart performer wilt in the heat. It took time and the employment of more sophisticated equipment before the technicians learnt how to jump from film to studio to long distance hook-up by wire. Cameras were large and had to be moved on rubber wheels by studio crewmen. Interchangeable lenses, allowing for a variety of shots (close-up, medium and so on) were unknown. And mistakes by actors or producers often led to hilarious results.

Peter Black, *Daily Mail* television critic, described one such incident in his book, *The Biggest Aspidistra in the World* (see Bibliography for details), in which the camera cables got twisted together on the studio floor and in an attempt to untangle the mess a technician inevitably plugged the wrong cable into the wrong camera. The result was that up above in the control room a distraught director was receiving pictures of Camera Two on Monitor One, which played havoc with his attempts to cue the sequence of shots!

Long before the advent of hand-held lightweight cameras and the use of film techniques in documentary and drama production, television fell back on stage and variety presentation for its format. Plays, as we have seen, often came live, direct from a West End theatre, and even where this was not the case, they were presented in the studio on a 'stage', complete with a

11

curtain that opened and closed between acts. Because there were no facilities for recording, actors had to move from set to set, which they managed with an agility that improved with practice. If a quick change was necessary, for example, from day clothes to night attire, the cameras had to fill in while the actor got out of one costume and into another.

It was during this era that BBC announcers wore evening dress and there were breaks between programmes during which an 'Intermission' card was shown on the screen and soft music played, while, presumably, thousands of domestic kettles were filled and loos flushed.

Television was meanwhile spreading nationwide, with five main transmitting stations that were boosted in 1953–54 by five further stations reaching outlying areas. Figures for television licences held show just under 400,000 issued in 1950, while this figure almost trebled two years later in 1952 as a result of the Coronation of Queen Elizabeth II, an event considered by many to have been the turning point in British television.

Curiously enough the event might never have been covered at all if earlier objections by the Earl Marshal, the late Duke of Norfolk, had not been overruled. It was felt that the cameras would be intruding on a solemn and sacred ceremony, but once the Duke's decision was reversed the royal event, like so many since, was literally re-vamped for television presentation.

Preparations took over a year and every available piece of equipment was pressed into service for what was then the longest single outside broadcast ever put out by the BBC. The main commentary was spoken by the late Richard Dimbleby and the ceremony was watched by an estimated twenty million viewers in Great Britain. It was also beamed to Europe over the fledgling Eurovision network. The timing was so exact, as Peter Black reported, that the actual moment of coronation was only two minutes out in the schedule.

It was the Coronation that early on earned Britain and British television a world-wide reputation for being able 'to do that sort of thing so well'. Another result was the fantastic rise in the sales of television sets, which rose by 50 per cent the following year. This upsurge was given yet another boost a couple of years later with the introduction in 1954 of ITV, and after this date television started to be taken seriously by the BBC: until then it had been overshadowed by radio (television programmes were still printed as a supplement to the *Radio Times*).

Before going on to examine the impact of Independent Television we should note that at this stage in the development of television Britain, America and Russia alone were providing a regular service, while French television began in 1949.

A second coming: the foundation of Independent Television

The first ITV company, Associated Rediffusion, went on the air in September 1955, and provided an alternative source of programmes from Monday to Friday for viewers in the London area. To get this far, however, had taken some six years of argument and counter-proposals, that were inevitably rooted in the post-war climate of a Labour-governed Britain.

We have seen that soon after the war the BBC revived its television service and was quickly back on the air, providing a mixture very much as before. The tone of broadcasting was very much that of the establishment and the influence of Reith was still felt along the corridors of Broadcasting House and Lime Grove.

But the post-war years engendered a feeling of change and voices, criticizing the monopoly position of the BBC, started to be heard. As so often happens with political questions that profoundly affect our lives, few people really cared about the moral and social questions raised by more television, and simply joined the clamour for a second channel. Their only hope was that this would not mean an increase in the licence fee (£2 at that time) and if a means could be found of providing more television hours through payments by advertisers then that was O.K. by them.

The Government of the day did not stand back, but in 1949 called for a major report on broadcasting and this was eventually published by the Beveridge Committee in January 1951. Curiously enough the Report recommended that things should stay much as they were, and rejected the idea of broadcasting supported by advertisers, or even the setting up of another public corporation to rival the BBC. It merely recommended

13

additional safeguards against abuse of the monopoly position of the Corporation, and made minor recommendations such as the setting up of regional councils.

There was one major dissenter in the shape of Mr Selwyn Lloyd, who stated in a minority report to the Committee that broadcasting should be handed over to commercial interests, with some safeguards, and even went so far as to look ahead to a similar system for providing an alternative radio programme service – which was not to come about for a further twenty years, in fact.

The Labour Government accepted the recommendations of the Beveridge Report and published a White Paper stating this fact in July 1951. However, a general election was held just four months later and on 25 October 1951 the Conservatives were elected in their place, with a firm pledge to reverse the proposals set out in the Beveridge Report, and this they did a year later in their Memorandum on Television Policy.

This period saw an intense amount of activity by pressure groups, both for and against television, supported by advertisers. One of the most influential exponents of the case for commercial television was a former BBC-TV controller Norman Collins, who had left the Corporation in 1950. He spent two years travelling up and down the country sounding out public opinion and putting over his theories about the alternative service and, with a group of impressive figures that included Sir Alexander Korda and the chairmen of Pye and EMI respectively, he set up the Associated Broadcasting Development Company. (Collins eventually became a director of ATV (Associated Television).)

Opinions about the proposed new television service were divided between the two major parties and their members. The Prime Minister, Sir Winston Churchill, appears to have adopted a 'sitting on the fence' attitude (at a time when his influence could probably have quashed independent television at a stroke) but finally came down in support of the commercial service. Some observers say this was the result of snubs by members of the BBC early on in the days of radio when Churchill wanted to broadcast propaganda about the General Strike. Politicians have long memories.

Lord Hailsham was against the idea of a commercial channel

and, in the House of Lords, Reith made his famous speech likening the advent of commercial broadcasting to 'smallpox, bubonic plague and the black death'.

Defeated in the 1951 election, the Labour Party now decided to fight back and opposed commercial television and, belatedly, the BBC also entered the fray. Various consumer groups also sprang up, among them the National Television Council, whose members included Lady Violet Bonham Carter, Lord Hailsham and Christopher Mayhew. Conservative back-benchers were on the whole in favour of breaking the BBC monopoly and the subject of television provided many lively exchanges at their Margate Annual Conference. For Labour, Clement Attlee pledged that his party would reverse any decision taken by the Tories to establish commercial television.

The final debate took place on 4 March 1954, and the Television Act (as it became the following July) was passed by 296 votes to 269. Although the bill has all the appearances of a measure that was steam-rollered through Parliament in the interests of party doctrine, the opponents of independent television were able to make their voices heard sufficiently to secure a promise that only spot advertising would be allowed on the new channel: there would be no sponsorship of programmes (as there was in America, for example).

The Independent Television Authority was duly set up, under the chairmanship of Sir Kenneth (now Lord) Clark, with Sir Robert Fraser appointed Director General. The Authority divided the country into twelve regions, for which fourteen independent contractors would supply programmes, the London franchise, for example, being divided between two companies. Some twenty-five groups applied for franchises. In addition to the fourteen programme companies, the Authority also oversaw the setting-up of Independent Television News (ITN) in which all the contractors have a financial stake. We shall be looking more closely at the functions of the ITA (now the IBA or Independent Broadcasting Authority) and ITN a little later on.

The first decade of commercial television witnessed two major events: the making of huge profits by the contractors (after some earlier losses) and a general decline in programme standards, which also affected the BBC.

The early profits certainly were staggering – a state of affairs summed up by the infamous remark of Lord Thomson, of Scottish Television, that a television franchise was 'a licence to print money'. Because advertising rates depended on large numbers of viewers, all pretence of standards went by the board and the commercial companies set about providing programmes that would attract the largest audience: as a result, serials, panel games and quiz shows became the staple diet during prime viewing time.

Unfortunately, the BBC was drawn into the battle for ratings – it has after all to justify periodic increases in the licence fee – so that it in turn had to lower standards in order to compete with the commercial channel.

The situation got so bad, in fact, that by 1962 another committee (set up two years previously) reported on the state of broadcasting; but although the Pilkington Committee castigated the companies for their low standards, the ITA chose to do nothing about them. Large profits were still being made, and the Conservatives, worried perhaps by the unacceptable face of capitalism, introduced a levy on advertising revenue, operating on a sliding scale from zero to 85 per cent.

The original franchisees were: Associated Television (ATV), Associated Rediffusion, Granada, ABC Television, Anglia, Scottish, Tyne Tees, Grampian, Southern, Westward, TWW, Ulster and Channel, and some of the smaller companies came on the air as late as 1960–61. The original contracts should have expired in July 1964, but although the ITA advertised for new applicants, none was accepted, and the fourteen companies were given fresh licences initially until 1967, and these were further renewed for another year, until July 1968. The delays were partly the result of the changeover from 405- to 625-line transmissions, and partly because of the possibility of a second channel being allocated to ITV.

We should note at this stage that certain technical developments had been taking place and, looking back as far as 1960, we see the introduction of telerecording using the Ampex system as we know it today. This had been developed in America, largely to assist programme companies to get over the problems of differing time zones, and the introduction of recording literally revolutionized the use of studios in this country. Rehearsals and shooting were no longer tied to transmission times and studio complexes became programme factories, able to turn out series and serials in blocks for later transmission.

1964 saw the introduction of BBC 2, transmitted on the 625-line UHF band (BBC 1 and ITV were still on 405-line VHF) and this became the Corporation's repository for serious programming. By this date – just over a decade ago – it is estimated that about 90 per cent of households had television, and the advent of the third channel gave yet another of those periodic boosts to television sales.

The next ITV re-shuffle occurred in 1968 when the present contracts (due – after extensions – to expire in 1976, but see below) were awarded, and some new companies took to the air. Applications for new licences had been invited as early as December 1966, by the ITA Chairman Lord Hill. By April the following year thirty-six groups had applied for the fifteen areas (the north had been split between Lancashire and Yorkshire, formerly covered only by Granada), and in July 1967 the winners were announced. There were some surprises.

Rediffusion, in London, disappeared to merge with ABC Television and become Thames (an uneasy marriage that seems to have worked), to provide weekday television for the London area. Weekends in the capital were to be covered by the London Consortium, the David Frost group, which would become London Weekend Television.

TWW, in Wales, disappeared without trace, to be replaced by Harlech Television. And the Yorkshire Telefusion Consortium took over in the north-east as Yorkshire Television. The remaining companies were (and still are until 1976): Anglia (covering the east of England); ATV Network (the Midlands); Border Television (the Borders and Isle of Man); Channel Television (Channel Islands); Grampian (North-East Scotland); Scottish Television (Central Scotland); Southern (south of England); Tyne Tees Television (North-East England); Ulster (Northern Ireland); Westward Television (South-West England); and Granada (Lancashire).

The programme companies vary considerably in terms of audience served, from Westward's 1½ million to the nearly 14 million shared by Thames (weekdays) and London Weekend.

The network tends to be dominated by the larger companies – London Weekend, Thames, ATV (with 10½ million Midlands viewers), Granada (8 million) and Yorkshire (6 million) – and, as we shall examine in due course, it is sometimes difficult for the smaller regional companies to get their programmes 'on the network'.

The 1968 shake-up was generally welcomed by the press and good things were expected from the new programme contractors, in particular from London Weekend, whose ambitious plans in the fields of public affairs and original drama seemed to promise the demise of the grey television weekends we had all been used to. However, a lot of things went wrong during that summer of 1968 when the new companies held their various opening nights. Harlech were first off, with a disastrous presentation by John Morgan introducing the Burtons with a mixture of familiarity and awed reverence that was acutely embarrassing to watch. Part of the transmission was blacked out through a technical fault.

A technicians' strike followed, and this affected Yorkshire, Thames and London Weekend and lost them an estimated £300,000's worth of advertising revenue. The BBC meanwhile was hugging itself with glee over the problems of its commercial rivals and, perhaps rather irresponsibly, went for an all-out attack on the ratings with a rush of popular programmes, with which it picked up between two and four million additional viewers.

The first year saw added problems for the new companies: they were hurriedly converting to colour, with mounting costs; and Yorkshire suffered another setback when their transmitting mast at Emley Moor, a new style concrete structure, collapsed in a storm.

Then in April, the Labour Chancellor, Roy Jenkins, surprised the companies by imposing a further levy on their advertising revenue in his 1969 Budget.

The companies were losing viewers and therefore advertising revenue, and in an unprecedented about-face in the autumn of 1969 decided to return to many of the old familiar programme formulae, a decision that coincided, rather unfortunately, with the publication by the 'Free Communications Group' of London Weekend's confidential application to the ITA which had won it the London franchise.

This was followed in September by the sacking of Michael Peacock, managing director of London Weekend, and the resignation of a number of key production staff. Very quickly, in fact, the company looked not at all like the one that had applied for and been granted the franchise. The situation deteriorated still further over the next two years, until the ITA, which up until then had remained curiously silent, was forced to take action. When Rupert Murdoch, owner of the *Sun* and *News of the World*, bought a share of London Weekend, the ITA announced that they might have to consider asking the company to re-apply for its franchise, as it had so changed since the date of the original submission.

A year after the Jenkins' Budget and following protests from the contractors, in March 1970 the Postmaster General announced measures to reduce the levy by some six million pounds; and this was followed by further concessions in 1971, under the Conservatives, with the appointment of Christopher Chataway as the new Minister of Posts and Telecommunications.

Meanwhile, under the guidance of their new chairman, Brian Young, the independent companies had been mounting a campaign to secure for themselves the fourth television channel, which they hopefully dubbed ITV 2. This idea was opposed by almost everyone who had a say in the matter – the Labour Party, the trade unions, the press, and members from either side of the House of Commons – with the result that Chataway was obliged to tell the companies firmly that it was definitely not on.

However, independent television managed to gain one concession: this was the ending of the restriction on broadcasting hours, so that television could now operate from early morning until later at night. This meant more opportunities to earn increased revenue from advertisers, but left the BBC with the problem of trying to compete to fill the day-time hours by making more programmes with the same amount of money that is available to them from licence revenue.

The current position

The BBC, as we shall see in the following chapter, is a body governed by Royal Charter, and in March 1973 it had its Fifth Charter, due to expire in July 1976, extended for a period of a further five years until 1981. The July 1968 ITV (IBA) contracts were, as we have seen, originally for six years, but in 1974 the Television and Sound Broadcasting Acts were passed, extending their life for a further two years until 1976. The IBA itself currently has a certain life only until 1979, and it has announced that it does not intend to put the current contracts up for offer in 1976 but retain the present contractors until 1979 (i.e. for eleven years in total since 1968). The Authority has however undertaken to review the present companies' performance and may issue directives as to their operation during the 1976–79 period.

Meanwhile the government enquiry into broadcasting has at last been set in motion, under the chairmanship of Lord Annan, and will be reporting in 1978. This report will affect the future of both sound and television broadcasting in the 1980s and 1990s in Britain.

The United Kingdom has capacity at present only for four television channels, and these are distributed between BBC 1 and 2, and Independent Television; the fourth channel remains idle. Without going into the complexities of engineering, the situation is complicated by the fact that the 625-line UHF service and the 405-line VHF service both still operate.

BBC 1 and BBC Wales have been broadcast for many years on 405 lines in Channels 1 to 13. These transmissions are likely to continue for several years, but they do not carry colour. Ninety per cent of the population can now receive BBC 1 and 2 on 625 lines and in colour (there are an estimated 6 million colour sets, and this figure has been increasing at the rate of a quarter of a million each month). All the 625-line transmissions are on ultra high frequency (UHF) using Channels 21–34 and 39–68, according to the area you live in.

The IBA is meanwhile continuing to extend its network of 150 UHF transmitters, which send out a duplicated black and white/colour signal on 625 lines. The original VHF network, opened in 1955, will remain in use until the Government decides to terminate 405-line transmissions. These VHF bands (numbered I and III) currently duplicate BBC 1 and ITV for the benefit of about 5 per cent of the population who still own

405-line-only television sets. These are usually located in remote and/or hilly areas – such as central Wales and north-west Scotland – and some 250 local transmitters are still required to bring the 625-line service to these viewers, to ensure a 100 per cent national coverage. Until this time, there can be no allocation of the fourth channel TV 4.

Broadly speaking, any future technical developments will come in the fields of broadcasting by wire and satellite, and in the development of video cassettes; and there are developments in the use of the existing television services for transmitting data in printed form. However, following the development of stereo in radio and colour in television, little change can be expected during the next twenty years or so in the realm of purely technical developments.

The future possibilities of television are examined in greater detail in the last chapter of this book, but suffice it to say at the moment that the development of wired television is likely to be slow because of the extremely high cost of laying co-axial cable and bringing it into people's homes, particularly when one bears in mind that the number of telephones installed in the United Kingdom is only 17·6 million (March 1973), spread across some 20 million households and additional business users.

Satellite communication calls for a high level of investment, and there is the additional problem of there simply not being enough room in space (they all have to be in the same orbit), Much the same can be said of video cassettes. Here the investment would be made by the viewer or consumer, but it is questionable just how much money the public has to spend. It is interesting to note, however, that today there are still only half as many motor cars or refrigerators as there are television sets!

What about the size of the television industry in Britain today? Television viewing is, regrettably, by far the most popular pastime and according to the Opinion Research Centre nearly half the population devotes most of its leisure time to viewing. Some 96 per cent of households own a television set and the average time spent viewing is around twenty hours a week or the equivalent time spent *in two and a half days at work*. Despite the battles for the ratings, viewership is roughly

21

spread between BBC and ITV, with average programmes attracting eight to ten million viewers, and special attractions such as the *Miss World Contest* or the *Eurovision Song Contest* being seen by twenty to twenty-five million people in this country alone. BBC 2 caters for some 5 per cent of the population and in this sense is truly a minority service.

In line with the increases in viewership, both BBC and ITV continue to put out more and more programmes: the BBC averages some 4,420 hours on BBC 1 and 2,550 on BBC 2 annually; ITV produces nearly 8,000 hours of television, taking the network as a whole. An interesting phenomenon at the end of 1974 and the beginning of 1975, was the reduction in the number of hours broadcast by the BBC for reasons of 'economy'. It might be argued that this amounted to little more than moral blackmail – until the Labour Government dutifully agreed to an increase in the licence fee to £18 for colour and £8 for black and white. Soon after this was announced, the IBA companies published their own plans for reductions in output, generally during weekday afternoons, to take effect the following summer, with several popular series such as *Crown Court* and *Emmerdale Farm* suspended for three months or more. The reason given was the fall in advertising revenue: a situation that cannot be cured as swiftly as an increase of the licence fee revenue in the case of the BBC.

With the increase in television hours has gone the increase in costs of getting programmes to the screen, with an hour of television roughly costing as much as £100,000 – probably as much as most of us expect to earn in a lifetime (and not in a lump sum, either!). To set up the fourth channel, either by BBC or ITV, it is estimated would cost some £30 million, and to do this must be added an annual running cost of some £20 million or more, depending on inflation.

Television is of course a major employer of people. The BBC (including radio services) employs some 24,000 people, and Independent Television about 11,000. To get an average programme on the air – the *ITV Yearbook* cites *Russell Harty Plus* as a typical example – takes around fifty people including six cameramen, six sound men, five props staff, five stage hands, electricians, carpenters, wardrobe and make-up staff, and various assistants: all this for a studio chat show.

Whether television should, or should not be allowed to continue to expand is a debatable point. The American experience clearly indicates that more is not necessarily better, and we shall return to this question continually throughout the course of this book.

Television abroad: the American experience

We cannot in a book of this scope examine television services all round the world and for an excellent volume on this subject the reader should consult the bibliography. However, it is pertinent to make comparisons between Britain and other countries, and because I have spent some time in both France and the United States observing the television services, I shall confine my remarks mainly to those two countries. Let us then first take a look at the situation in America.

Television in the United States can best be described as a merchandizing rather than an entertainment medium. And the very size of the industry is somewhat mind-boggling. There are nearly 700 commercial television stations, which are supported by some £1,500 million's worth of advertising annually. The largest television advertiser, Procter and Gamble, spend annually the equivalent of the BBC's total budget, while the combined profits alone of the three major networks exceeds this figure and is the same as the total revenue of the French service.

Over sixty million households own a television set, and of these half have colour sets and over a third have more than one set. With a choice of ten or more channels in some urban areas, and programmes being transmitted from early morning until the early hours of the next day, it is not surprising that viewing hours have increased steadily, so that, as one observer remarked, an American college student has spent half as much time again in front of the television set as he has in the class-room. Average viewing is as high as thirty hours a week.

The Federal Communications Commission which (loosely) controls the television industry allows direct ownership of no more than five television stations, and the three major networks – CBS, NBC and ABC – between them own fifteen stations and are associated with literally hundreds of affiliates.

23

CBS owns stations in New York, Chicago, Los Angeles, St Louis and Philadelphia and has diverse interests that include publishing and films, cassettes and baseball, which bring in an annual income of over £400 million. It has around 200 affiliated stations, who take most of the CBS networked programmes.

NBC, itself an industry giant, is a subsidiary of RCA, a vast equipment manufacturer, owner of Hertz car rental, and heavily involved in defence contracts. The company owns stations in New York, Chicago, Los Angeles, Washington and Cleveland, and has more than 200 affiliates.

ABC, the third network, owns stations in New York, Chicago, Los Angeles, San Francisco and Detroit, and has a modest 172 affiliates.

American television is financed by advertising, which comes in the form of sponsorship of entire programmes or programme segments, or from spot advertisements. Affiliates of the major networks, who agree to take a proportion of programmes from their network chief each week, receive a share of the network advertising revenue, and add to this what they can make from the sale of local spots. Advertising is limited to six minutes during prime time (7.00 to 10.00 pm) and twelve minutes outside this time, in any one hour, but these figures are often exceeded, with commercial breaks appearing every seven or eight minutes during the programme. Americans have fought back by purchasing muting devices which cut off the sound during the commercials by remote control.

Because of the dominance of advertising, programmes are planned with the sponsor in mind. As a result only 'safe' themes are allowed, so that several weeks' observation of American television gives one the impression of a steady diet of *Bonanza, The Lucy Show* (some so old they are still shown in black and white) and re-runs of ancient movies, of which as many as 150 can be found in one week in a major urban centre with ten or more channels to choose from.

Most programmes originate from the networks, though they may be manufactured for them by independent contractors. These latter are frequently based in California and the demand for television filler material has revived ailing studios, such as Universal, which now churn out hundreds of episodes and 'filmlets' annually. To succeed, a programme must be networked on upwards of a hundred stations to start to recover its costs.

Another important element in US television is the timing of programmes to earn most money, and this is invariably during the evening period, when the rate for one minute's advertising can go as high as £35,000 or more – as against a modest £4,000 to £5,000 during the daytime.

Not unnaturally the 'success' of a programme (and this, in fact, means a series) is judged by its position in the ratings, and new programmes launched at the start of the autumn/ winter season that do not make it within a matter of weeks are ruthlessly chopped early in the new year to be replaced by fresh offerings or re-runs of tried and trusted formulae from the past.

The most popular type of series is the soap opera, and many of these are seen in Britain and around the world: *Bonanza* has been sold to over eighty countries. The formula rarely changes: police, FBI, situation comedy, cowboy shows, quiz and chat shows, the occasional 'spectacular', with the result that, on the whole, the diet is boring and unappetizing. Characters are stereotyped, overplayed so that even those with minimal intelligence will get the message, with stock roles being adopted by the good guys and the bad guys: the rebellious teenager or the cop with the heart of gold who really dislikes his job.

In the battle for the ratings, there is sadly little room for serious documentary or comment programmes, and the proportion shown on American television is probably less than a twentieth of that broadcast in Britain. There are occasional breakthroughs, though, and while in America I watched a whole evening's programming given over to an examination of the energy crisis. Even the commercial breaks were confined to one every thirty minutes, which on American television seemed like a miracle.

Recently, too, some major advertisers have turned to sponsoring serious documentaries as part of their public relations and institutional advertising programme, but it is still a strange experience for the Englishman to hear that the news programme has been brought to you by the makers of 'X Brand'. The major news programmes, and these often take up to an hour or more in the early evening period, are slotted outside prime time, but the coverage of local and national news is good, if a little

25

dramatic. Each network has its resident anchor man, a policy that has led to unheard-of salaries being earned by men like Walter Cronkite of CBS and John Chancellor of NBC.

Public reaction against so much that is bad in American television has assisted the development of an educational and public service channel. Allowance for such a service was made by the Federal Communications Committee twenty years ago, and gradually some 200 mini-networks have grown from university and community television services. A further boost was given in 1967 following the report of the Carnegie Commission, which led to the setting up of the Public Broadcasting Corporation. It is on this network that many of the BBC's successes have been shown, including the *Civilisation* series and *The Forsyte Saga*, attracting a whole new class of viewer who would normally not watch television at all (estimated at as much as a third of the population), and an audience of some 30 to 40 millions a week suddenly started to take a new interest in television.

These developments give observers some slight cause for faith in the future of American television, which for so many years has existed with the finest technological know-how simply being under-used because of the demands of the market place. This process has naturally led to an egress of talent from the industry – what genuinely creative person wants to turn out hours and hours of *Marcus Welby MD* or yet another episode of *Mannix* or *Ironside* – and a general lack of faith in the medium on the part of the averagely intelligent citizen. It is surprising that even the advertisers have not realized that by being a little more subtle and forcing the networks to put out programmes that appeal to something a little higher than the lowest common denominator they could attract a whole new, influential audience, instead of simply counting faces in front of television screens.

It is true that corporation heads call for breakdowns of the audience for particular shows and ideally it should be an audience with the greatest purchasing power: urban, white, college educated, and aged between twenty and fifty! But by putting out the sort of programmes they do, the networks appear to be shying away from any real attempt to capture the interest of just this cross-section of the community.

26

American colour television works on their own NTSC system (jokingly referred to in the trade as 'Never the Same Colour') and generally the technical quality is poor, with frequent changes in tone as the picture switches from programme to commercial spot or from film to videotape to live transmission. This necessitates constant adjusting of the set which can quickly drive a British viewer insane.

Television in France

French television is the largest public service broadcasting organization in Europe. It has three networks, two in colour and one in black and white, the latest of these being initiated in 1972. The service is state owned, financed by licence fees, but pulls in additional revenue from advertising. This is restricted to a few minutes a day, and its very scarcity raises its saleable value.

In January 1975, the television system switched to a service of three nominally independent channels, each in competition with the other. The two major channels are *France 1* (FR. 1) and *Antenne 2* (A 2), with a third minority channel that reaches a tiny proportion of the country – yet to which the government has granted public access!

The French had developed their own colour system, SECAM, which has been adopted by Russia and the satellite countries, but rejected in favour of the German PAL system by Britain and most other European countries. America operates on a third system, NTSC as noted, but special conversion equipment allows for interchange of programmes between the varying systems.

Until 1968, under De Gaulle, the French service (ORTF) was firmly under government control and the President made full use of the news services to put out Gaullist propaganda. Matters came to a head during the troubles of May 1968 and a strike by journalists forced television off the air for over a month, apart from a daily news bulletin. One of the first tasks of the new President, Georges Pompidou, was to introduce certain reforms of the ORTF and greater freedom for broadcasters. Eventually most of the strikers, and those who had been sacked under the previous regime, were reinstated. The

ORTF now employs some 14,000 staff and operates from a massive new complex on the Left Bank. The Eiffel Tower is used as a transmission mast.

Although state owned, the service suffers from many of the worst defects of American television. I observed French television during a period of seven months and was amused at the fascination with technology at the expense of creativity in programming. By this I mean that while one Sunday afternoon, for example, all the programmes on one channel were broadcast from an express train, the *Aquitaine*, which broke a speed record between Paris and Bordeaux, this truly remarkable feat of electronic engineering did not of itself do anything to raise the quality of the programme content. But this obsession with television hardware is often carried to extremes, as British viewers of the *Tour de France* cycle race each summer will recall: cameras are mounted on motorcycles or slung from helicopters, all in the cause of realism.

These engineering feats would be acceptable if French television had a tenth of the creative drive of the French cinema. For all the months I viewed I saw little or no original modern drama, for example. And so much of what was shown was simply not television material – concerts, two or three hour long debates, incestuous discussions about the role of television itself. All these items could just as well have been presented over one of the radio channels, and television left to broadcast something more *visual*.

There are a number of British and American imports screened, including *The Saint*, *The Avengers* and *Ironside*, dubbed in French. There are a number of parlour games and quizzes. There is a lot of talk and serious music. Much of the presentation is amateurish, particularly the staging of variety shows, as any viewer of the *Eurovision Song Contest* will recall. A talk programme I regularly watched was transmitted live from a smart restaurant in central Paris: a good idea but unnecessary, as the clatter of dishes often effectively drowned the voices of the speakers. Sometimes interviews were conducted outdoors in parks or on the roofs of buildings, recalling localized American small-budget programmes or even BBC's ghastly lunchtime offering from Birmingham, *Pebble Mill at One*.

There is also a lot of unnecessary competition between the

two major channels, who send out duplicate teams of camera-men and reporters to cover the same news event. This is clearly wasteful of money and talent and reminds one of stories that where *Time Magazine* or *Newsweek* will send two men, *Paris Match* will have eight!

Conclusions

From this brief survey of the television services in Britain, America and France, I think we can conclude that – in the immortal words of critic Milton Shulman – Britain has 'the least worst television in the world'. Many things are not right with British TV, as we shall be examining in the following pages, but we have the advantages of greater choice, more freedom from government or commercial pressures, and a wider range of creative abilities in a position to make use of television than either of the other two countries put together.

2. The BBC: Its Constitution, Licence Fees and Administration

Introduction

Broadcasting by television and radio in Britain is regulated by the Minister of Posts and Telecommunications, under the various Wireless Telegraphy Acts 1949–1967 (which prohibit the sending or receiving of radio communications except by licence). Two bodies are in fact licensed to provide television and radio services currently, and they are the British Broadcasting Corporation and the Independent Broadcasting Authority (formerly the Independent Television Authority). We shall examine the latter body in the following chapter.

The BBC, as we have seen, operates two television services – BBC 1 and BBC 2 – and in addition provides four national radio services and operates twenty local radio stations. It also broadcasts to countries abroad through its External Services. Users of television sets must obtain an annual licence, which is bought through the Post Office, and at the start of 1975 a licence for black and white television cost £8 annually, and £18 for colour. In June 1974, there were 11·5 million black and white television licences issued, and a further 5·9 million for colour. Various unofficial estimates put the number of clandestine television receivers, operating without licence, at between one and two million, but dealers are now obliged to notify the licensing authority when they sell or install a new television set.

Both the BBC and the IBA are required to provide a public service with the purpose of disseminating 'information, education and entertainment' and the constitution and finances of the BBC are governed by their periodic Royal Charters and by the Licence and Agreement of 1969. Both bodies are independent authorities in so far as concerns the day to day running of their broadcasting operations, but Government exercises ultimate control through the Minister of Posts, who is answerable to Parliament on questions of policy and may issue directives on some technical and other subjects to the BBC and IBA.

Both organizations, again, are expected to show a sense of balance and impartiality in their presentation of programmes, particularly where matters of public policy and controversial topics are concerned. And it is in this area that the Minister has power to prohibit the broadcasting of any particular item or type of programme, and ultimately to revoke the licences of either body at any time. However, no formal veto has been applied in the history of broadcasting to any particular item.

Both the BBC and the IBA are required to prepare annual accounts and these, together with their reports, are presented to Parliament. They are available for the public to read in their respective annual handbooks.

The BBC consists of twelve Governors, including a Chairman, a Vice-Chairman and separate national governors for Scotland, Wales and Northern Ireland. Governors are appointed for a maximum period of five years by the Queen on the advice of the Government. The Governors are advised by a number of committees who examine and report back on such subjects as education, the social impact of television, music, religious broadcasts, and so on. The Governors also appoint the chief executive of the BBC, the Director General, with whom they discuss top level matters of organization and finance. The Director General is chairman of the BBC's board of management, which includes his chief assistant, the managing directors of television, radio and external services; the directors of programmes for television and radio; and directors of personnel, finance, public affairs and engineering.

Additionally the National Broadcasting Councils of Scotland and Wales control the policy and content of television (and radio) programmes for their respective areas.

We have seen that the BBC's income comes from the licence fee. Its domestic services are financed by an annual grant voted by Parliament which is in fact the income from the sale of licences, less some expenses for administration. In 1973–74 this net sum amounted to £141 million. This figure is supplemented by income from certain BBC trading activities, including the sale of *Radio Times* and other magazines and records (through BBC Publications) and sales of programmes to countries overseas, through BBC Enterprises. About 75 per cent of the total income is spent on television.

Most nationally networked BBC programmes originate in London, though some do come from the regional centres in Scotland, Wales and Northern Ireland, and eight other studios in main centres.

Output on BBC television 1973–74

	Hours	% of total
Programmes produced in London	4,966	46·2
Programmes produced in Regions	3,918	36·5
Films and imported material	1,245	11·6
Open University programmes	618	5·7
Total hours broadcast	10,747	100·0

Pattern of BBC television production 1973–74

Current affairs, features, documentaries	1,879	23·1
Sports programmes	984	12·1
Children's programmes	607	7·4
Light entertainment	552	6·8
Drama	501	6·1
News	417	5·1
Schools programmes	360	4·4
Further education	261	3·2
Religion	162	2·0
Music	109	1·3
Programmes in Welsh	78	1·0
Continuity (announcements, trailers)	376	4·6
	6,286	77·1
Imported series, films	1,245	15·3
Open University	618	7·6
	8,149	100·0

(Note that totals do not tally because of repeats, etc.)
Source: *BBC Handbook 1975*.

BBC 2 (in spite of what the Corporation may say officially about it) is the minority interest channel, which additionally has to carry the programmes for the Open University. BBC 1 carries general interest programmes, competing fiercely with ITV, and broadcasts some sixteen hours a week of schools programmes. Programmes that originate on BBC 2 are sometimes re-shown on BBC 1.

During 1971–72 the BBC sold some 7,000 hours of programmes to eighty-six countries overseas.

Most BBC productions come from the main studio complex at White City in west London and from other studios located in the capital. There are additional regional studio centres in Belfast, Birmingham, Bristol, Cardiff, Glasgow and Manchester; and further studios at Aberdeen, Bangor, Edinburgh, Leeds, Newcastle, Norwich, Plymouth and Southampton.

Both the BBC and IBA are members of the European Broadcasting Union which manages Eurovision (see Chapter 4 below), and the BBC also belongs to the Commonwealth Broadcasting Conference. It is also a partner in Visnews, which supplies a service of world news to some 150 television services in eighty-six countries; and a member of Intertel (International Television Federation) which exchanges other programmes with overseas countries.

The BBC Charters

The First Charter came into being on 1 January 1927, after Parliament had considered the report of the Crawford Committee on the infant radio service, and lasted for ten years. Another committee re-examined broadcasting in 1935, under Lord Ullswater, and confirmed the BBC's entry into international broadcasting through the Empire (later World) Service. A Second Charter was granted also for ten years, and this entrusted the development of the national television service to the BBC, after the report of the Selsdon Committee of 1934.

The Third Charter was granted in 1947, and renewed to 30 June 1952, when a Fourth Charter came into being (following the report of the Beveridge Committee) which introduced commercial television as an alternative to the BBC. 1964 saw the granting of the Fifth Charter, after publication of the report of the Pilkington Committee, and allowed the BBC to borrow money for the first time in its history; it also extended the areas of influence of the Broadcasting Councils for Scotland and Wales.

Five years later a Supplemental Charter was granted as a result of the passing of the Post Office Act of 1969, when the Post Office became a public corporation. In March 1973, the government extended this Charter until July 1981, and it is in this context that the BBC now operates.

The full text of the Royal Charter and the Licence and Agreement can be read in the 1974 edition of the *BBC Handbook* (pp. 285 *et seq.*).

One of the main provisions of the BBC Licence concerns the need for the Corporation to refrain from 'editorializing', that is, to refrain from expressing a point of view on any matter of public policy or public controversy. The BBC maintains its position of impartiality by means of balance. At first this was taken to the extreme, in the sense that every programme dealing with a controversial subject had to be balanced within itself, so that all sides of a question were heard together. This was felt to be less helpful than putting forward a convincing argument and the policy now is to achieve balance overall, over a period of time or through a series of related programmes.

There has never been any attempt to balance the content of the news. News is very much an arbitrary and uncontrolled phenomenon: an event happens and it is reported, as being newsworthy. There may be of course a certain amount of *censorship* (which we will examine later) – by omission, by inclusion, by emphasis, by the placing of news stories in bulletins, and by conflicting opinions as to what is newsworthy. The latter is very much an editorial decision, and editors, being human, are not always impartial.

The BBC is at pains to point out that impartiality or neutrality does not mean to imply that it will never speak out on issues, and clearly there are whole subject areas (oppression, poverty, injustice, etc.) where programme makers have put over a point of view.

The Governors

The BBC is headed by a Board of Governors, and the present

Chairman is Sir Michael Swann, a former university professor from Edinburgh. The remaining Governors present an image of establishment respectability and are drawn from what we call 'public life', with a tendency towards obscure peeresses from the remoter parts of the country. Their occupations include solicitor, company director, landowner, university don, civil servant and one ex-TUC chief, Vic Feather.

The BBC's advisory councils

The *BBC Handbook* reports that during the year 1972–73 the corporation had the advantage of consultation with no fewer than fifty-five advisory bodies, though many of these (including the twenty regional radio councils) apply mainly to sound broadcasting.

'Together,' the Report goes on, 'they constitute a major element in the system by which the BBC maintains a close relationship with its public; other means include Audience Research, regular analysis of correspondence from viewers and listeners, a methodical study of all that is said in Parliament and the Press on broadcasting matters, and the daily contacts which the Governors and staff of the BBC, at all levels, have with people outside.'

Obviously the BBC takes its job seriously, but when I find that correspondence with Broadcasting House frequently goes unanswered and fellow writers complain to me of the impossibility of breaking into the inner ring of programme planners and producers, I question just how in touch the BBC really is with the public.

Let us look more closely at some of these advisory bodies.

They fall into two main groups: those that are invited to advise on BBC policy in a general kind of way and over a wide area; and those dealing with more specialized areas. The first group includes the General Advisory Council, of some sixty members, drawn again from a wide range of areas of 'public life'; and then there are the Northern Ireland Advisory Council, the Broadcasting Councils for Scotland and Wales, and the eight English Regional Advisory Councils. (In addition there are the twenty Regional Radio Councils as already mentioned.)

The second group comprises a number of specialist bodies

35

and they advise on such matters as charitable appeals, educational broadcasting, music, religion, science and technology, engineering, and so on.

How are people recruited to these bodies? The BBC offers the following answer: 'The selection of men and women to serve on these bodies is made after a process of external and internal consultation, reinforced in many cases by the BBC's own direct knowledge, acquired through its own multifarious contacts, of persons likely to have a valuable contribution to make.' Can I hear the anguished cries of readers who feel they have expert knowledge to offer but have never been consulted?

The membership of the various advisory bodies currently numbers some 850 people – 'the vast majority of whom are, or have recently been, engaged in some form of public activity. . . . Between them they cover a wide cross section of the national life and represent to a substantial degree, the BBC believes, the voice of informed and responsible public opinion . . .'! (*BBC Handbook 1974.*)

The General Advisory Council numbers sixty members and meets about four times a year. The agenda for these meetings is settled in advance by a smaller business committee, consisting of the chairman and nine members, which meets more frequently (eight times a year on average). Full meetings of the Council are attended by the Chairman and Board of Governors of the BBC, and other senior management staff.

Most subjects discussed or reported on are presented in the form of papers, and in the year under review these included an examination of the Council's own role and suggestions that the BBC should from time to time publish pamphlets on general broadcasting matters (the first of these appearing in February 1973 entitled *Taste and Standards in BBC Programmes*).

Occasionally specific programmes that have aroused comment, for example an episode of *Till Death Us Do Part*, are brought in for discussion.

In addition, there are a number of Regional Advisory Councils. These include Northern Ireland, with a membership of twenty, with representation on the General Council. The eight English Regional Councils, with fifteen or twenty members each, cover East Anglia, the Midlands, North, North East, North West, South, South West and West, and the chairman of each Regional Council is *ex officio* a member of the General Council. Subjects discussed usually centre on those raised by the General Council, to which the Regional Councils add a local flavour, and their comments, recommendations or criticisms are fed upwards into the General Council by way of the regional chairmen.

Coming to the specialist councils, they appear generally to carry more weight. In the field of education, two main bodies operate: The School Broadcasting Council for the United Kingdom and the Further Education Advisory Council. The former body numbers some forty members, drawn from the professional teaching associations, local education authorities, and the Department of Education and Science, and it is they who in fact design the curriculum of radio and television broadcasts for schools. Everything which the BBC broadcasts to schools has in fact been commissioned by them.

The Further Education Advisory Council has thirty members and makes recommendations to the BBC about further education programmes, both on vocational and non-vocational courses.

There are separate Schools Broadcasting Councils for Scotland and Wales and a Sub-Committee for Northern Ireland, and various sub-committees exist to examine particular areas and make recommendations.

Similar functions are performed by the Central Religious Advisory Committee, with twenty-nine members, including laymen, which advises the IBA as well as the BBC about religious programmes. The Central Music Advisory Committee, under the chairmanship of Lord Harewood; Central Agricultural Advisory Committee; Central Appeals Advisory Committee; Engineering Advisory Committee; Science Consultative Group; Programmes for Immigrants Advisory Committee; and the Advisory Group on the Social Effects of Television are all concerned with the areas defined in their titles.

The BBC publishes a full list of members of its advisory bodies and, glancing through these, certain names tend to stand out. Membership of the General Council includes Mr Campbell Adamson, Jack Ashley MP, Sir Stanley Rous and Moira Shearer. While committees dealing with religion and education are bristling with bishops and canons and professors and teachers. Members of Parliament are well represented in all the groups, and there is a generous sprinkling of OBEs, particularly when one gets down to the level of local advisory committees.

Are these people representative – and if so, of what? I tend to think they are not particularly representative. Success in 'public life' appears to be almost the sole criterion for membership of these bodies. I feel that the adoption of this criterion means that a certain amount of talent can well be overlooked that could be drawn on – particularly from among writers and intellectuals and people engaged in publishing and other media. The committees seem to attract a certain type: the sort of person one would find on the board of governors of a local grammar school or sitting on the bench as a JP. Beyond being pillars of the establishment I do not think they necessarily have anything useful to say on the subject of television and I suggest that their very 'respectability' precludes their viewing of much of what is actually broadcast over all three channels.

BBC organization and staff

The BBC employs approximately twenty-four thousand people, of whom 13,566 are classified as programme, technical and executive staff, and 11,316 as manual, secretarial and catering. This situation gives rise to the argument that for everyone actually producing something for television or radio, there are two people administrating.

Sitting on top of this vast organization, as we have seen, are the Chairman and the Board of Governors; and just below them comes the full board of management, which includes various senior staff such as the managing director for television and his equivalent in radio.

The managing director for television has under him the following departments:

Engineering Operations and Maintenance (Television) Programme Groups and Departments, including:
 Planning
 Presentation
 Drama Group
 Light Entertainment Group
 Outside Broadcasts Group
 Current Affairs Group

Features Group
Documentary Programmes
Music Programmes
Children's Programmes
School Broadcasting
Further Education
Religious Broadcasting
Purchased Programmes
Open University Productions
Programme Servicing Departments, including:
   Film Operations and Services
   Design Group
   Studio Management
   Scenic Services Group
   Artists' Contracts
   Script Unit
Administration, including:
   Liaison
   Co-productions
   Television Enterprises
   Television Computer Projects
Finance
Personnel

Each of these sections is then broken down still further, with divisions between BBC 1 and BBC 2, and such further sub-groupings as 'Comedy, Light Entertainment, Television' and 'Plays, Drama, Television' and 'Science Features', 'Arts Features', 'Music Programmes', and so on.

The very size of the BBC tends to give it a certain remoteness that is not shared, for example, by independent television which employs less than half the people (11,000) dispersed among fifteen programme contractors and the IBA head office and branches. So it is not surprising that there is more person-to-person contact inside the smaller ITV companies than between a BBC television features producer and the Chairman of the Board.

The size of the BBC inevitably creates hierarchies and political sub-groupings, which appear to be common in other media-oriented professions, notably newspaper and magazine publishing, where politics, one journalist commented to me, takes up something like 75 per cent of the working day.

One advantage of size, though, is that individuals have an opportunity to get on with the job, and normally only have to refer decisions upstairs when in doubt. And while the BBC likes to talk of itself as a cohesive body, it should be borne in mind that it is a vast and complex organization made up of thousands of individuals who do not necessarily think and act alike.

As can be seen from the foregoing breakdown of BBC television departments, a number of them are concerned with services for programme productions. One of these, by way of example, is the Scenic Services Group. The BBC has the biggest design department in the world, which employs around a thousand people in groups dealing with design, costumes, make-up, and scenery. These are then constructed by another thousand staff, employed in the workshops. Together the departments spend some £4 million annually, most of it in connection with drama presentation. But in spite of this, more than half the work goes to outside contractors and freelances. Some productions can require seven or eight hundred props to mount them, from carpeting and furniture, to pictures and ornaments.

Two important service departments are those concerned with artists' contracts and payments for use of copyright material. The Programme Contracts Department assesses fees for those participating in programmes, and these range from a (very) few pounds to fees paid to top 'stars'. Some two hundred thousand contracts are negotiated annually and the department also handles labour permits for foreign artists and administers the dozen or so BBC orchestras and bands. Relations have to be maintained with performers' agents and with the main unions, including Actors' Equity, the Musicians' Union, the Radio Writers' Association and the National Union of Journalists.

Copyright fees are paid for commissioned music and scripts, and additional fees are paid to the main copyright protection agencies – the Performing Rights Society, the Mechanical Copyright Protection Society, Phonographic Performance Ltd, the Publishers' Association and the Society of Authors. The BBC normally pays an initial fee for use of copyright material covering a single performance, but with optional rights, subject to payment of further fees, to repeat programmes or sell them to overseas contractors.

Production is also divided into various departments. These

are: Drama Group, which is organized into three sub-groups dealing with single plays (e.g. *Play for Today*), drama serials (e.g. *War and Peace*) and drama series (e.g. *Colditz, Barlow at Large*). The Current Affairs Group is similarly divided, with separate units concerning themselves with such programmes as *Nationwide* and *Panorama*. The Sports and Outside Broadcast Group deals with sporting (e.g. the Cup Final) and non-sporting events (e.g. State Openings of Parliament) and some light entertainment programmes.

The Light Entertainment Group itself is divided into Variety (e.g. *Cilla Black, Morecambe and Wise*) and Comedy (e.g. *Steptoe and Son*). The Features Group looks after General Features (e.g. *Man Alive*), Science Features (e.g. Dr Bronowski's *Ascent of Man*) and Arts Features (e.g. *Omnibus*), while specially filmed documentaries (e.g. *The Search for the Nile*) come under the Documentaries Department. Television News is the subject of a special department that supplies material for both BBC 1 and BBC 2. Links between programmes and trailers on either channel, the weather forecasts and phone-ins are handled by the Presentation Department.

The BBC also owns and operates quite an amount of real estate, and in the case of television this is generally located in west London, close to the Television Centre at Wood Lane, W12. The building was opened in 1960 and was the first pur-pose-built television complex in the world. It has seven major colour studios and accommodation for up to 550 artists in dressing rooms. There are separate presentation suites that co-ordinate programme contributions from all sources, in-cluding outside broadcasts and other studios (such as the news studio at Westminster). The international control room handles input via satellite and links such as Eurovision. Two further studios are set aside for television news and the separate scenery block occupies about one acre. Further studios are located at Shepherds Bush where the Television Theatre caters mainly for light entertainment shows; at Lime Grove, where current affairs programmes are produced. Television camera crews are based at a separate complex at Ealing, which also handles editing and dubbing of completed film.

There are of course several regional production centres, already referred to, and a whole network of transmission and

41

relay stations dotted about the country. Additionally the BBC maintains a number of overseas offices, both for the sale of programmes and to house news correspondents. Some of these (e.g. Paris) have their own sound studios.

The licence fee and BBC income

BBC income comes from a share of the licence fee (after deduction of some expenses) and from sales of programmes and publications. Gross licence fee income for the year 1972–73 was £137·6 million, an increase of £16·2 million on the previous year. The increase is partly the result of the spread of colour television, though the cost of collection and certain other Post Office expenses (including tracking down evaders) rose from £8·1 million to £11·7 million, leaving the BBC with a net income from licences of £125·9 million. To this can be added the figure of £1·7 million contributed by BBC Enterprises. At 31 March 1973, the BBC had a surplus of £1·1 million.

Of the total income to the BBC of £124·5 million, nearly £82 million was spent on television programming. A breakdown of expediture on television production for the year ended 31 March 1973 is as follows:

	£'s million	% of total
Production and other staff costs	43,246	52·8
Artists, speakers, copyright, film, recording and design materials	26,926	32·9
Rental of circuits	1,919	2·3
Power, light and heating	1,716	2·1
Building and plant maintenance	2,201	2·7
Rent, rates and telephones	2,804	3·4
Transport	1,186	1·5
Other expenses	1,897	2·3
Totals	£81,895	100·0

Few details are given of payments of salaries, though the Chairman receives only £6,000 and the Vice-Chairman and some other Governors even less (£2,000, and in some cases £1,000). There are only eighteen employees in the £10,000 to

£12,500 a year bracket, and only one person earning more than £17,500 per year. These salaries are modest in comparison with the pickings to be had in the professions and some areas of industry.

The 1974 licence fee was £7 for a black and white television and £12 for colour. The separate radio-only licence fee was abolished in February 1971. The annual licence fee has increased from £2 in 1946, to £3 in 1954, £4 in 1963, £5 in 1965, £6 in 1969, and £7 in July 1971.

The British television licence is one of the cheapest in Europe, as the following table shows:

	B/W	Colour
Denmark	£23·01	£36·03
Norway	£23·70	£31·11
Sweden	£20·95	£30·48
Finland	£12·63	£23·16
Germany	£16·59	£16·59
Netherlands	£11·36	£11·36
Italy	£8·16	No service
Eire	£7·50	No service
(At June 1973)		

BBC publications and enterprises

The BBC earns additional revenue from its own publications, notably the *Radio Times* and *The Listener*, and from a variety of trading operations classified as BBC Enterprises.

Radio Times is published in twenty-six editions and its programme pages give details of all radio and television programmes. There are additional feature articles, usually linked to programmes and personalities. Its circulation is the highest for any British periodical at four million, with a claimed readership of eleven million.

The Listener is a more serious broadcasting journal, with a circulation of some forty thousand copies weekly. There are sometimes transcripts of whole programmes in it, articles by producers and other specialists, book, music and cinema reviews, and reviews of television programmes that include those put out by ITV.

Other general publications are linked to programmes (e.g. on subjects like 'Do It Yourself' or 'Keep Fit'), and others, more specialized, relate to further education series, mainly language subjects, or school books related to educational programmes, details of which are sent in advance each autumn to schools, so that teachers can plan their curricula. Over 12½ million items are purchased by some 33,000 schools every year.

There are also a number of publications related to overseas broadcasts, such as *London Calling*, which gives details of broadcasts and other information. BBC Publications are located at 35 Marylebone High Street, London W1.

BBC Enterprises is in fact a group of departments operating in both home and overseas markets and selling programmes and associated products to other users. The unit is more than self-supporting and in fact contributes to the Corporation's overall budget.

The BBC is one of the world's largest producers and sellers of programmes overseas and some 7,000 hours of programmes are sold to ninety countries abroad. Based at Ealing, the department has branch offices in Sydney, Australia, and Toronto, Canada, while sales to the United States and South America are handled by Time-Life Films, in New York.

The current sales by BBC Enterprises reached an all time record when Peter Dimmock announced in March 1974 that turnover was up by 38 per cent and these had brought in a record £4·5 million, including $5 million from the United States and Latin America.

Some 200 titles are now available on BBC records, tapes and cassettes and in the autumn of 1974 the BBC launched its own 'Beeb' pop label. Films and other recordings are also available for hire to schools and other groups using 16mm projectors and 1,500 items are available for sale and 300 for hire. Spare film footage, newsreels of past events and other stock film is sold or hired to film makers and users, and the BBC has the world's largest film library.

A special merchandizing department looks after the marketing of BBC properties associated with programmes, licensing their use in books and publications. The facilities unit, finally, hires out studios and equipment for the manufacture of film and television productions by other users.

The BBC and the public

As well as keeping its finger on the pulse of public opinion through its numerous advisory bodies (though we have questioned the effectiveness of these in practice), the BBC has several other formal and informal channels for communication between itself and its audience.

Investigations into the size and make-up of the audience for BBC programmes are carried out on a continuous basis by Audience Research, a department with more than thirty years experience in the field. Using a running survey of listening and viewing, some 2,250 people are interviewed *daily* (i.e. 70,000 per month; 800,000 per year) and questioned about what they listened to on the radio or watched on television. The results are collated from the various regions and localities – full and part-time interviewers work in their home areas throughout the country – and brought together in the daily audience barometer, which itemizes every programme broadcast nationally and indicates its audience figure.

In order to gain some idea of the quality of the audience as opposed to mere numbers, the BBC uses a number of listening and viewing panels, the membership of which totals 6,000 people. Each week, panel members receive questionnaires relating to the coming week's broadcasts, and they are invited to comment on these, but urged not to alter their normal listening or viewing habits to do so. The opinions gathered in this way are then condensed into a series of reaction profiles, comparing one programme with another.

Other surveys and investigations are carried out, not all of them after a programme has been broadcast. For example, a producer of a new series might ask audience research to take a sampling to find out the public's existing knowledge of a particular subject, in order to assist him in pitching the programme content at roughly the correct level.

The BBC also receives a certain amount of spontaneous reaction to broadcasts, either from organized pressure groups concerned with certain subject areas, comments in the media or from public figures, and more directly in the form of unsolicited correspondence from the public, which sends letters of praise or complaint to the Corporation at the rate of some 2,000 daily.

45

Other ways of keeping in touch with the public include programmes involving requests (mainly on radio), visits to BBC premises and participation in programmes as members of the studio audience and lectures to interested groups by members of BBC staff.

For those interested in working for radio and television, the Programme Contracts Department holds regular auditions in music, drama and variety; and play and talk scripts, music scores, etc., can be submitted to the appropriate editors, nationally and regionally. Advice in these fields is contained in the BBC's own booklet *Writing for the BBC*.

The BBC obviously maintains a number of other quite large departments as part of its organization, and these include an engineering department, which I feel is outside the scope of this book. Some of these departments we shall be looking at more thoroughly when we come to examine the various programme structures – news, sport, religion and so on – in succeeding chapters.

That then is the skeleton structure of the British Broadcasting Corporation: the flesh and organs are comprised of the people who work there. For the vast majority of the population, there is no need or desire for contact with this vast, anonymous body. But for those, such as myself, whose work touches upon the affairs of the Corporation, contact can be a chilling experience. Without personal, informal contacts with programme staff it is almost impossible to track down individuals and as already noted a lot of correspondence simply does not get answered. When tackled about this, a nameless BBC voice informed me tartly that 'they couldn't possibly reply to all the letters they received'. If this is in fact true, then there is a serious case of remoteness from the customer. It is also almost impossible to extract information from departments: telephonists appear to be trained to demand of the enquirer 'are you just a member of the public?' I have had to confess on more than one occasion that, yes, indeed I am, and the frosty silence with which this is greeted is sufficient to deter all but the most assiduous researcher.

3. The Independent Broadcasting Authority

As we have seen, since 1954 with the creation of the Independent Television Authority (ITA), the public has had an alternative television (and, more recently, radio) service to that broadcast by the BBC. ITA's name was changed in 1973 when the Authority became involved in commercial radio, and it was re-named the Independent Broadcasting Authority.

The IBA has four main functions in relation to television: selection and appointment of the programme contractors; supervision of programme planning; control of advertising, largely through the Code of Practice; and the transmission of programmes.

The IBA, as can be seen, does not make or produce programmes, although at the time of setting up the independent television service this could well have been the formula adopted. When we come to examine the possibilities for making use of the eventual fourth channel, we will see that proposals have been made that an independent programme body, similar to the BBC, should be set up that would make programmes centrally.

Programme making is in the hands of the fifteen ITV contractors, and Independent Television News (ITN) in which each of the contractors has a shareholding.

The Chairman, Deputy Chairman and nine members of the Authority are appointed by the Minister of Posts and Telecommunications, and the policy of the Authority is guided by the provisions of the Independent Broadcasting Authority Act of 1973 (which consolidated previous sound and television broadcasting acts).

Major policy developments are discussed at meetings held twice a month. The Chairman of the Authority keeps in day to day touch, through the Director General of the IBA. Previous chairmen have included: Sir Kenneth (now Lord) Clark from 1954–57; Sir Ivone Kirkpatrick from 1957–62; Lord Hill of Luton from 1963–67 (when Harold Wilson switched him to the BBC). The present Chairman, Lord Aylestone, has held the position since 1967.

A life peer, Lord Aylestone was formerly Mr Herbert Bowden, and served as MP for Leicester until 1967. He held a number of ministerial posts, including Leader of the House of Commons from 1964 to 1966, and then as Secretary of State for Commonwealth Affairs. The present members of the Authority are: Mr Christopher Bland, the Deputy Chairman, who has had mixed experience with the GLC, the Local Government Training Board, the Whitley Council, and the Conservative Bow Group. Mr W. C. Anderson comes from the unions (general secretary of NALGO, the local government union) and Dr T. F. Carberry from the civil service and the University of Strathclyde. Mr Glyn Davies was a director of education. Stephen Keynes is a merchant banker. Baroness Macleod of Borve is the widow of the late Iain Macleod, a former chancellor, and was created a life peeress in 1971. She is a JP; Mr Alexander Page is chairman of the Metal Box Company. Two recent appointments are those of Mrs Helen May Warnock, a former headmistress and author of books on existentialism; and Professor J. Ring, a research scientist, specializing in astronomy.

There have been only two Director Generals, the first of whom was Sir Robert Fraser. He was succeeded in October 1970 by the then unknown Brian Young, former headmaster of Charterhouse and a director of the Nuffield Foundation.

All told, the IBA employs some 1,300 people at its headquarters in Brompton Road, and in its regional offices and transmitting stations. Also included in the 1,300 are 750 staff at Crawley, which houses the finance and engineering divisions. These figures do not include the staffs of the contracting companies, which employ from 500 to 1,500 people each, according to size.

The ITV system

From the start of independent television in 1954, the ITV

system has been planned as both plural and regional. The Act of 1954 required the Authority to do all it could to ensure an element of competition in the supply of programmes divided between a number of companies. It also stipulated that a proportion of each company's output should be basically regional in content and appeal. As a result, two distinct principles have been established. First, that programmes seen by a viewer in any one place would come in fact from a number of different contractors (i.e. a Granada production screened by Thames in London); and second, that a proportion of programmes would be produced by the companies primarily for showing in their regions alone – such as the various nightly magazine programmes.

These principles, the workings of which we shall be examining as we go along, were clearly stated by Sir Robert Fraser at the time of his retirement in 1970: 'The Authority at the time regarded its decision to construct the network on a plural, co-operative and internally competitive basis as the most fundamental of its decisions.'

The argument is that because television production is costly in terms of finance, technical and manpower resources, only some of the regional companies should have special responsibility to produce a larger number of programmes than the others. The Authority therefore created a series of major network companies – originally four, but now five – whose task is to originate most of the programmes taken by the whole network. Meanwhile the smaller companies would be primarily concerned with productions geared to the specific needs of their particular viewing areas.

The major companies are currently: London Weekend and Thames in London, Granada in Manchester, Yorkshire in Leeds and ATV in the Midlands. In theory, the system should not preclude the smaller regional companies from 'getting on the network' but in practice it appears that the smaller companies often have difficulty in doing this. Because the major companies are located in prosperous catchment areas and attract the bulk of the revenue from advertising, they are in a stronger position to mount and network programmes and series. The smaller companies, being weaker financially, cannot introduce new programmes without an opportunity to screen

49

them over a large part of the network, with the result that there is little innovation, and the product of the major companies, whatever its standard, tends to dominate the independent television network, whether this was the deliberate intention of the Authority or not.

Some of the smaller companies have fought against this state of affairs by specialization, which in other areas of business is quite often the salvation of the smaller enterprise. So that while ATV can afford to mount elaborate variety programmes for ultimate sale to the United States, many original documentaries and feature programmes start from Anglia or Southern Television.

We have already noted that the de-restriction of television hours has favoured the independent companies, by placing them in a position to earn still greater revenue from extended advertising.

How are the contractors selected? The Authority, in the words of its annual report, 'has preferred a diversified and multiple control of ITV programme companies to a concentrated or single ownership, and has further preferred that regional companies should be regionally owned. This is a reflection of the Authority's policy of seeking to shape the institutions of Independent Television in such a way as to increase the diversity and number of the nation's means of communication . . . in the selection of programme companies the Authority has sought to provide a broad balance of interests within the Independent Television system as a whole and to ensure that the control and ownership of each company forms an identity and character likely to provide a balanced and high quality television service and in the case of regional companies genuinely reflects the area served.'

Unfortunately this pious statement of intent does not always work out in practice, and although 1968 provided something of a reshuffle, some major interests would seem to have an all-pervading influence in many aspects of independent television. The 1968 awarding of contracts saw the elimination of TWW, to be replaced by Harlech; the formation of Yorkshire Television, to take over part of the previously Granada-owned territory; the alteration of the time division in the London area between the two contractors; two existing companies

(ABC and Rediffusion) hastily married together to form Thames, the weekday contractor for the capital; and two companies formerly providing split-week services appointed to serve one area throughout the week (Granada and ATV – as consolation prizes for the loss of Yorkshire and part of London, respectively).

One could point, however, to the dominance in television of the Grade/ATV/EMI complex, with their multifarious interests in talent agency, films, publishing, records, etc., which is considered unhealthy by some observers. Or to the diversification into publishing and motorway cafés and television rental by the Granada Group. Or to the fiasco surrounding the launching and establishment of London Weekend Television in London, a company that has undergone so many organ transplants as to be hardly the body that applied for and was awarded the franchise.

The programmes screened in any one ITV area can come from three sources. In the first place, they may be produced by the local contractor from its own resources, and mostly these take the form of regional news and magazine programmes. The second source of material is the purchase of programmes from outside the ITV system, and this includes cinema films (British and foreign) and series or serials made by foreign television companies. Limits are, however, placed on the amount of foreign material that can be screened and this is currently 14 per cent of the output. (Most viewers probably have the impression that it is more.)

The third source of material is that which comes from the major network companies listed above and from ITN. Some of the companies deservedly have a better reputation than others for the quality of their output, and although Granada is responsible for *Coronation Street*, it also has a high reputation for original plays and series, and serious talk and discussion programmes. Yorkshire television does well with plays and documentaries, but was also responsible for the execrable *Stars on Sunday*. ATV produces a number of mid-Atlantic spectaculars and some drama. Thames, a matey little station, produces good plays and features. London Weekend . . . well, what can one say? Apart from sports output, which is excellent, and the current affairs programme *Weekend World* (which is viciously chopped during the summer months), little in the way of original production emanates from the South Bank.

ITV companies submit quarterly schedules to the Authority, showing their intended weekly output for the months to come. A proper balance has to be struck if the schedule is to be approved, and alterations may be made, including the calling in and examination of actual scripts. Special emphasis is laid on the needs of children and the Authority stipulates that certain programmes can only be shown after 9.00 pm, when children are assumed to have gone to bed. All programmes are monitored, so that they may be examined after transmission, and retrospective judgements may be passed by the Authority and communicated to the contracting companies. But it is the responsibility of the latter to ensure that the provisions of the Act are carried out.

To arrive at a certain level of co-operation and liaison a number of committees exist, drawn from the staffs of the IBA and the programme companies, the main one of these being the Standing Consultative Committee. This meets once a month at the Authority's headquarters and is presided over by the Chairman of the IBA, and it is attended by the principal contractors.

The Programme Policy Committee is similarly constituted but its major functions are to let the IBA inform the companies of its views on programme policy generally and to establish the main trends for future planning of programmes.

The bulk of the in-fighting takes place on the Network Programme Committee, and it is here that the major companies carve up the viewing hours among themselves and hear suggestions from the smaller contractors anxious to gain a showing on the network. Two representatives of the Authority also sit on this committee, and there are several sub-committees dealing with more detailed questions. The Programme Controllers Committee meets weekly to determine the make-up of the network part of programmes, and membership is confined to IBA staff and representatives of the five major contracting companies.

The actual staff of the IBA is divided into seven main groups: Programme Services (control and supervision of programme output); Administrative Services, divided again into the

secretariat and the establishment department (personnel and
trade union affairs); Finance (handling budgetary control and
forward estimates); Engineering, sub-divided into six departments, including Station Design and Construction, Station
Operations and Maintenance, Network and Service Planning,
Network Operations and Maintenance, Experimental and
Development, and Engineering Information Service; the Radio
department looks after the affairs of commercial radio; Advertising Control (supervises amount and quality of advertisements); and, finally, Information.

The finances of the IBA

The Independent Broadcasting Authority needs money to meet
its running costs – largely the provision and maintenance of
transmitters – and to operate the various controls required of
it by the state. Separate financing now operates for television
and radio. Revenue comes to the IBA through the programme
companies, who pay a rental to the Authority for use of the
television transmitters. The programme companies, in turn,
rely for their income on the sale of advertising time, out of
which a levy is paid to the Exchequer and the cost of making
programmes is financed. Broken down, the income of a typical
programme contractor shows that 97·0 per cent of its total
comes from the sale of advertising, with only 3·0 per cent
accruing from ancillary activities. The pattern of the contractors'
expenditure is as follows:

Programmes	42·1%
Supporting departments and services	10·7%
Rental paid to IBA	8·6%
Allowance for depreciation	3·5%
Exchange Levy	13·9%
Corporation Tax	8·5%
Surplus (for capital expenditure, reserves, dividends)	12·7%
	100·0%

Income from the programme companies to the Authority
totalled some £13 million in the year ending March 1974, plus
a further £560,000 from other sources. The pattern of the
expenditure looks like this:

53

	£ million
Network operations and maintenance	5,103
Planning, construction and development	1,689
Programme and advertising control	725
Depreciation	1,546
	9,063
Taxation	3,856

Over the past ten years the Authority's income has increased overall from £6·2 million in 1964 to £14·1 million as of March 1973 with a drop to £13·9 million in March 1974. Operating and capital expenditures have risen accordingly – £3·0 million to £12·1 million, though capital expenditure also includes some provision for replacement of existing equipment for a higher cost as and when this becomes necessary.

It has been noted that part of the programme companies' income from advertising is paid over to the Exchequer in the form of a levy, though discussions were initiated to change this method of treatment to a levy on profits (rather than on income), and this took effect from June 1974. Whatever method is used it is not likely to reduce the amount of money paid by the companies to the state, in the opinion of the Authority.

Since the levy was introduced in 1964, the programme companies have paid over some £217 million to the Exchequer: this is in addition to normal taxation, calculated (since 1954) at around £173 million.

Technical operations

A large part of the IBA operation is concerned with the establishment and maintenance of the complex transmitter network. Between them the independent companies operate some fifty studios, which are linked, via Post Office cables, to over 150 transmitters. Each of these represents a capital investment of about £350,000 for each channel.

As well as building and owning the transmitters, the IBA sets the technical standards of programmes and monitors the contractors' output to check technical quality. Since the start of ITV colour in November 1969, facilities have been extending all the time to include colour on the 625-line network. This has brought a corresponding increase in television hardware owned by the companies – 240 colour camera channels, 80 colour video recording machines, 90 colour telecine machines (for transmitting film), 20 colour outside broadcast units, and so on.

Mention has already been made of the continuing extension of the UHF television service throughout the United Kingdom and, parallel with the BBC development, the IBA has been adding transmitters and relay stations at the rate of 45 each year, and this figure is likely to increase to 70 per year. Many of these new stations are designed for unattended operation.

Establishment of a new transmission station is a complicated business, from the initial selection of the site (after extensive field tests) and obtaining the necessary planning permission from the relevant local authority, to the ordering and acceptance of the necessary buildings and equipment. Operation and maintenance of the transmitter network is in the hands of some three hundred engineers, who work closely with those from the Post Office. Another department also works with the Post Office on booking the necessary line links provided by them for the linking of transmissions between studios, outside broadcasts and other events. Because fifteen contractors are involved (plus ITN) the process is necessarily complicated.

In the field of research, IBA engineers are working on a number of developments. These include DICE (digital intercontinental conversion equipment) that adjusts American standard television images to those of Britain and the Continent. The prototype unit has been installed inside the headquarters of Independent Television News. A further development of DICE will convert European pictures to American standards.

Another development is in the field of broadcasting the written word – news flashes, stock exchange prices, etc. – by means of ORACLE (optional reception of announcements by coded line electronics), and viewers can observe evidence of this in the small dots that appear above the screen when the height control is lowered on domestic television receivers (in the London area only at the moment). Eventually it should be

55

possible for a viewer to press a button on a control unit and call up a 'page' of information for viewing on his television screen.

Maintenance and attention to breakdowns is the responsibility of a team of mobile engineers based within a comfortable two hours' drive of each of the main transmitting stations. Records show that on average breaks in transmission account for 0·023 per cent of total broadcasting time, or two minutes in every 150 hours.

Advertising control (see also Chapter 9 below)

The Independent Broadcasting Authority controls the quantity, distribution and content of advertising on independent television (and radio). No precise rules have been laid down. The Independent Broadcasting Authority Act of 1973 (which consolidated previous Acts) simply states that 'the amount of time given to advertising in the programmes shall not be so great as to detract from the value of the programmes as a medium of information, education and entertainment'.

Since the start of ITV transmissions in 1955, the Authority has allowed a maximum of six minutes of spot advertising per hour, *averaged over the day's programmes*. A further rule restricts the maximum to seven minutes in any clock hour for television, and nine minutes for radio.

Because programmes may overrun slightly and advertisements are normally inserted particularly around the end of one clock hour and the start of another, the IBA allows a certain amount of flexibility in placing of commercials, but any excess occurring in one hour is counter-balanced by a reduction somewhere else.

Control over the *distribution* of advertising breaks is exercised in three ways:

When programme schedules are submitted to the Authority for approval (see above), allowances for commercial breaks are also negotiated with the Advertising Control Division, and it is here that the flexibility described above is allowed within certain precise limits.

Adjustments of the break schedule have to be agreed if there is an alteration to the programme schedule (e.g. a last minute programme is inserted as a result of the death of a statesman). All such changes have to be agreed in advance.

Finally, the IBA conducts a weekly inspection of the statistical report supplied by Audits of Great Britain (AGB), the service that records the actual minutes and seconds of paid advertising that are broadcast by the commercial companies throughout the day.

In contrast with the American practice of allowing frequent short(er) advertising breaks, the IBA favour fewer longer breaks. In practice, these average three breaks per hour, each of two minutes during an hour-long programme. When programmes change on the half hour, advertising breaks are inserted between them, and sometimes at the fifteen minute break. Wherever they occur, advertising breaks must come at a natural point in the programme – half-time during a football match, at the end of an 'act' in a play – and, in fact, writers for commercial television can use the anticipated commercial break as a significant theatrical device similar to the break between acts on the legitimate stage.

Certain programmes and types of programme are not allowed to carry commercial breaks of any kind. These include: certain current affairs and documentary programmes, including *This Week* and *World in Action*; schools programmes and half hour adult education programmes; religious programmes; some early evening children's programmes; formal royal ceremonies and appearances of the Queen and Royal Family; and in any programme lasting less than twenty minutes.

In programmes of more than twenty minutes and up to forty minutes, one natural break of up to $2\frac{1}{2}$ minutes is normally allowed. A few sixty-minute plays and documentaries are also restricted to one break only. In programmes of more than forty and up to seventy minutes, one natural break of 3 minutes or two of $2\frac{1}{2}$ minutes are allowed, depending upon the nature and timing of the programme.

In programmes of more than seventy minutes and up to a hundred minutes' duration, two breaks of up to $3\frac{1}{2}$ minutes or three of up to $2\frac{1}{2}$ minutes are allowed. In boxing and wrestling programmes and other programmes of more than a hundred minutes the distribution of the advertising breaks should be designed to best serve the interests of the presentation (i.e. between rounds in boxing).

The practical effect of these regulations is that the number of intervals at the beginning and end of programmes and in natural breaks is on average fractionally less than three per hour. During the 35 hours from 6 to 11.00 pm in a typical week there would be 54 programmes with a total of 98 advertising intervals, 48 of which are *between* programmes and 50 *within* programmes.

Taking the whole of an average week, in which 180 programmes are broadcast, 100 of these will have no internal advertising break; 60 have one break and 20 will have two.

Successive advertisements must be recognizably separate and must not be arranged or presented in such a way that any separate advertisement appears to be part of a continuous feature. Nor must the sound level be greatly in excess of the normal programme content level.

There are over 20,000 new commercials each year. Of these, 15,000 come from small local advertisers, and are made up of five or seven second spots, simply presented (still slide with voice over). The remaining 5,000 advertisements come from the large manufacturers of branded goods, among them all the well-known household names.

Control of advertising quality

In addition to the fifty or more Acts of Parliament that regulate advertising, among them the 1968 Trade Descriptions Act, the IBA lays down its own code of advertising standards and, not unnaturally, is more concerned with prevention of offensive advertising reaching the screen than taking punitive action after the event.

The main concern of the Authority, therefore, is to exclude any advertisement that is thought to be misleading, and to decide which types of advertisements should be excluded altogether, from both television and radio. Guidance in this area is provided by the Minister of Posts and Telecommunications, advertisers and their agencies, who subscribe to a voluntary code of practice, and two major advisory committees: the Advertising Advisory Committee and the Medical Advisory Panel.

Under the Independent Broadcasting Authority Act, 1973, the IBA is required to appoint 'a committee so constituted as to be representative of both (i) organisations, authorities and persons concerned with standards of conduct in the advertising of goods and services (including in particular the advertising of goods or services for surgical or medical purposes) and (ii) the public as consumers, to give advice to the Authority with a view to the exclusion of misleading advertisements . . . and otherwise as to the principles to be followed in connection with the advertisements.'

The Chairman of the Committee is independent of any advertising, financial or business interest and the committee has to be consulted by the Authority on the drawing up of a code of practice and any subsequent amendments or recommendations to this. The committee numbers ten members (including the chairman). Two members are particularly concerned with medical advertising, and are drawn from the British Medical Association and the Pharmaceutical Society; four members come from advertising bodies (Advertising Association, Institute of Practitioners in Advertising, Incorporated Society of British Advertisers, and a committee of press and periodical interests); the three remaining members are women, and regarded more or less as consumers. The members serve as individuals, and not as elected representatives of the various bodies that may, in fact, have nominated them.

The 1973 Act also requires the IBA to appoint a Medical Advisory Committee, whose functions are threefold: to advise on,

'(a) advertisements for medicines and medical and surgical treatments and appliances;

(b) advertisements for toilet products which include claims as to the therapeutic and prophylactic effects of the products;

(c) advertisements for medicines and medical and surgical treatments for veterinary purposes,

and such other advertisements as the Authority may think fit to refer to the panel.'

The IBA consulted the twelve professional associations concerned with medicine, and as a result appointed a panel of seven consultants in general medicine, pharmacology, chemistry, dentistry and veterinary science; and an additional four consultants in paediatrics, gynaecology, dermatology and ear, nose and throat disorders. The second four are consulted by the original seven should the need arise.

The advisory panel considers not only advertisements for medical and surgical products, but includes in its scope toilet articles, disinfectants, shampoos, etc., which include therapeutic claims for the product. 'The panel in effect has been "licensing" the purposes for which acceptable medicines could be offered with reasonable safety in television advertisements in the light of its members' expert knowledge and experience of the formulae involved and of general medical opinion about their use' (*IBA Handbook*).

Other less formal panels are consulted about products in other areas, such as financial services, motor oils, cleaning products, electrical goods and other products, for which specific claims are made and which would be difficult to assess without the benefit of expert advice.

In spite of this elaborate system of checks, 'offending' advertisements still slip through. In February 1975, following an article in the *Observer*, Cavenham Ltd agreed voluntarily to withdraw two of their television advertisements for Marmite. The *Observer* piece had pointed out that Marmite contained 11·5 per cent salt and examined possible dangers of its being fed to small babies, in the light of a government report on baby foods that recommended that babies should not be given additional salt in their diets and were in fact already in danger of over-consuming salt simply from the milk they drank.

The IBA Code of Advertising Standards and Practice

The IBA Code has been drawn up in consultation with the Minister of Posts and of the various advisory bodies listed above. It is a lengthy document, with thirty-four main provisions, and four appendices, three of which cover Children, Financial Advertising, and Medicines and Treatments. The fourth appendix lists the various other statutes that control advertising (from the Accommodation Agencies Act, 1953, to the Trustee Savings Bank Act – some fifty acts are cited).

Let us first look at some of the general regulations. Some of these concern the identification of advertisements and lay down the principle that 'an advertisement must be clearly distinguishable as such and recognizably separate from the programmes'. Situations and performances must not be used in such a way as to be reminiscent of programmes, and although, for example, farming products may be advertised inside a farming programme, the advertisement cannot refer to the programme.

Certain formulae cannot be used, such as the 'news flash', and subliminal techniques are banned. Political, religious and charitable advertisements are also excluded en bloc. Other unacceptable products and services include breath testing devices, matrimonial agencies and correspondence clubs, fortune tellers, undertakers, unlicensed employment bureaux, betting tipsters, private detectives, and, of course, cigarettes and cigarette tobacco.

Advertisers must not attempt to appeal to fear or superstition to sell their products, nor should they be presented in such a way as to mislead, as, for example, the use of glass or plastic sheeting to simulate the effects of floor or furniture polishes might do.

'Knocking copy' is out; that is, making unfair comparisons with other products or services. Further regulations cover inertia selling, competitions, schemes for home work, instructional courses, mail order advertisements, and direct selling. A number of words also cannot be used, and they include 'guarantee', 'warranty' and 'free', without further submissions to the Authority, and in the case of the word 'free' unless goods and samples are in fact supplied at no cost to the consumer (other than actual postal or carriage costs).

The regulations concerning advertising and children contained in the first appendix are broadly divided into two sections – the child audience and the use of children in advertisements.

Advertisements directed at children must not encourage them to enter strange places or converse with strangers (to collect coupons, vouchers, or labels) nor appeal to the child's sense of duty and loyalty or encourage a sense of inferiority should he not purchase the product. And where a free gift is offered, it must be portrayed in relation to another object so that it is easy to determine its actual size.

The use of children in televised advertisements is regulated in a number of ways and subject to the employment regulations.

Children in advertisements 'should be reasonably well mannered and well behaved' and considerations given to the portrayal of safety: children must not appear unattended in street scenes, or be shown to disregard the normal highway safety regulations. Nor should they be shown climbing up to high shelves, on cliffs, or trying to reach for a product on a table above their heads. Children must not be shown using certain objects – medicines, cleaning materials, matches, petrol, gas, electrical appliances and many others. Also they should not be shown driving or riding upon agricultural machinery. And where an open domestic fire is shown on the screen in the presence of children it must have a fireguard 'clearly visible'.

Financial advertisements are similarly regulated in the second appendix, which covers investment and savings, prospectuses, insurance, lending and credit, financial information and commodity investment (this latter category is totally forbidden). Further regulations govern the content of such advertisements, and stipulate that, *inter alia*, entertainers and sportsmen cannot 'purport to be directors, officers or other employees of an advertiser' nor may they 'present, endorse or recommend any investment offer'.

Professional entertainers may not endorse medical products (this is in the third appendix) and the advertisements may not be presented by doctors, nurses, etc., in such a way as to imply professional endorsement or recommendation. A whole range of products and services is excluded in this category, and includes: contraceptives (other than officially sponsored family planning services); smoking cures; products for the treatment of alcoholism; contact lenses; hair and scalp treatment clinics; products for the treatment of piles; slimming clinics; and pregnancy testing services. Certain other product categories are banned, such as treatments of illnesses that require professional medical attention, offers of diagnosis by correspondence, and claims that any product can extirpate any illness or ailment.

Copy must not be exaggerated and remedies must not be described as 'natural', 'magic', 'miraculous', etc. Nor must products imply that they will increase one's sexual virility, while advertisements for bust developers are not permitted. Advertisements for treatments of hair and scalp disorders must not imply that they will do any more than arrest the loss of hair and no product appealing to women must imply that it will induce miscarriage. Finally a whole series of illnesses and disorders are specifically itemized, and the advertisements for products claiming to cure them are prohibited. These last include such obvious cases as cancer, cardiac symptoms, chronic rheumatism, tuberculosis and many others.

Television sets are found in some seventeen million households in the British Isles, and for the cost of a single advertisement, a manufacturer can reach many of these. Advertising rates vary from short, regional announcements (five or seven seconds) to elaborate film and videotape productions, lasting thirty seconds or more, networked nationally during prime time. Here the cost goes up, to around £6,500 for thirty seconds, or £1 for every 1,200 homes – and this without production costs.

Out of every ten advertisement scripts submitted, two have to be revised after examination by the IBA. We will examine how censorship works out in practice in Chapter 9.

The ITV programme mix

In addition to controlling the quantity and quality of advertising, the Independent Broadcasting Authority exercises a certain amount of control over the structure of programmes and their content. Because there are fifteen contractors and many programmes one only reads about in regional editions of the *TV Times* or the annual handbooks, it is not easy to get a clear picture of output as a whole except by reference to IBA statistics.

The contractors produce some 8,000 hours of programmes annually in their own studios, a weekly average of 156 hours. Nearly two-thirds (i.e. 100 hours) of this self-made output is classified as *serious* and includes news and news magazines, current affairs and documentaries, religion, education and a proportion of the children's programme output. The rest of the material broadcast consists of drama (which can sometimes be serious), entertainment and music, and sport.

During the evening period from 6.00 to 11.00 pm, about 29 per cent of the time is devoted to serious programmes – though it will be found that many of these occur before 7.00 pm and after 10.00 pm, and can really be said to appeal to an audience consciously looking for serious programmes. Total weekly programme output has been steadily increasing from 47 hours in 1956 to over 100 hours at the end of 1973, and along with this overall increase the amount of serious programming has also risen: from $9\frac{1}{4}$ hours in 1965, $16\frac{1}{4}$ hours in 1969 to 36 hours today.

Imported programmes, as we have already seen, are restricted to 14 per cent of total transmission time, but this is a high figure in view of the low quality of so much imported material, particularly that from America. It should also be pointed out that cinema films (British and foreign included) account for *as much* transmission time as current affairs and documentaries, or entertainment, and *more* than all sports output or all educational programmes.

Because of the influence of the network companies – the Big Five – much of the companies' output is seen only regionally and not nationally. At the end of 1963, as much as 65 per cent of ITV's total production (5,000 hours out of 8,000) was seen only regionally. At the same time fully or partially networked programmes numbered only 450 hours annually.

Even the IBA admits that this sort of situation could be considered 'wasteful in narrow economic terms'. But 'the Authority believes there are great advantages in regional diversity'. Apart from localized news magazines dealing with regional issues, I fail utterly to comprehend what these supposed advantages are, and given that it takes fifty technicians to mount a Russell Harty programme, this duplication can only be described as thoroughly irresponsible and profligate.

Clearly the arguments of regionalization do not apply in practice to the purchase and transmission of old films, and some observers have pointed out that these are often spread around the network and transmitted at different times and on different days to deliberately falsify the ratings. These observers further argue that if screened nationally (instead of piecemeal) old films would top the ratings, and no production company wants to see its own home produced output superseded in this way.

In 1973, the *Sunday Times* published a guide to films on television, with ratings from 'Cancel all other arrangements' down to 'Ring up and complain': unfortunately many of the films available fall into the latter category. It is a frightening prospect to learn that some 20,000 films are theoretically available for screening – and this figure excludes, among other things, all foreign language films(!) and made-for-TV items, largely from America! Excluding these items, the average ITV week will include at least half a dozen old films.

We will return to this question in Chapter 8.

Violence on television

Some control over the amount of violence shown in independent television programmes has always been exercised by the Authority, largely through the recommendations contained in its ITV Code. This was formally applied from 1964 and established the 'family viewing' concept, so that after 9.00 pm 'children' were assumed to be in bed and after this time responsibility for what they view rests with their parents rather than with the broadcasters. A working party was set up in 1970 to further examine the portrayal of violence on television, and in October 1971 a revised code of violence was published.

The revised code made many of the points outlined in previous documents: that there is no alternative to the assumption that the portrayal of violence has a harmful effect upon individuals and upon society. There was no evidence that violence in a 'good' cause was less harmful than other kinds, nor that 'sanitized' or 'conventional' violence was any less harmful. They also concluded that violence portrayed as happening a long time ago was equally harmful: 'horror in costume remains horror'.

Certain guidelines are therefore laid down, both for the inclusion of violent scenes in drama and fiction, as well as its factual reporting in news and documentary programmes. The main recommendation is that what is shown should not go beyond the bounds of what is tolerable for the average viewer, that it should not be psychologically harmful, and that the violence portrayed should not be of a kind readily imitable by the viewer.

The Code admits that it cannot make universal rules, and that the programme makers must carry the responsibility for their own decisions. One might well question: do they? The portrayal of sex and violence in the cinema has become almost universal, with the result that patrons either become immune or simply stay away. Television is more powerful, because it is there, uninvited inside the home. Many observers feel that the level portrayed is intolerable and we shall examine their views in Chapter 7.

IBA audience research

The Broadcasting Act enjoins the IBA to make arrangements for 'ascertaining the state of public opinion concerning the programmes broadcast by the Authority' and this it does, in fact, in a number of ways.

Information about the size and composition (age, social class, etc.) of the audience is provided for ITV by Audits of Great Britain Ltd (AGB), through the Joint Industry Committee for Television Advertising Research (JICTAR). Automatic electric meters are attached to television sets in some 2,650 homes throughout the United Kingdom, and these record on a minute by minute basis whether the set is switched on and to what channel it is tuned. This of itself cannot guarantee that anyone is *watching*, and in addition the households selected are asked to keep a special diary which records in quarter hour periods the details of those watching. This comparatively small sample is the basis for compiling the 'ratings' indicating the popularity (or not) of television programmes.

Information about the audience for schools broadcasts is obtained on a co-operative basis with the BBC, through their Schools Broadcasting Council.

Audience profiles are regularly published by the Authority, and at a glance they indicate that the bulk of the ITV audience is aged forty or over, and predominantly in the C2 and DE classes. Apart from sports programmes, significantly more women and children watch television than men. Teenagers generally are minority television viewers.

It is not sufficient to know simply how large the audience is for any programme, and Opinion Research Centre Ltd now operate a panel of 1,000 viewers in the London area, who record daily information about what they view and their comments on the programmes. In 1973, the survey was broadened to include

66

opinions gathered in the regions (in rotation) through a postal survey, based on 2,000 electors in each ITV region.

This research is backed up by a number of *ad hoc* surveys and in recent years these have included a two year research project into the viewing interests of children, undertaken by ORC in conjunction with the Centre for Television Research at the University of Leeds. During 1973, an investigation was conducted into religious programmes.

Systematic analysis of all the data gathered is undertaken for the IBA by the firm ASKE Research Ltd. One of their findings reported that the more a programme was appreciated the more a viewer was likely to watch it in succeeding weeks!

The Authority also contributes towards research in general terms into the effects of mass media, and in 1963 contributed a grant of £250,000 towards the establishment of the Centre of Mass Communications Research at the University of Leicester.

Independent Television News

Independent Television News (ITN) is a non profit-making company that is jointly owned by all the programme companies and controlled by a board of directors representing those companies. The Director General of the IBA normally attends ITN meetings, and the appointment of the ITN editor has to be approved by the IBA.

ITN is responsible for the news service put out by the independent companies, including the well-known *News at Ten*, and news programmes at 5.50 pm and the lunchtime news (*First Report*). It also mounts news programmes of major events such as space flights and international crises, coverage of the Olympic Games and general and local election reports.

ITN is based at Wells Street in Central London, close to the Post Office tower, and is fully equipped for colour operation using both the European PAL and American NTSC systems. It has two studios and an outside broadcast unit, telecine and VTR, and complex laboratory facilities for processing all types of news film.

ITN is a joint owner along with United Press International and Paramount of UPITN, a new film agency that makes daily shipments of news film to over a hundred overseas television stations.

Independent Television publications

This is the publishing arm of independent television, and is owned by the companies jointly. ITV Publications is responsible for the publication of the programme guide *TV Times*, which sells some 3¾ million copies weekly; *Look-In*, for younger readers; and the monthly *TV Life* which started publication early in 1974, with a curious mixture of showbiz schmaltz and the airing of various actresses' sexual hang-ups that scarcely recommended it as family reading.

4. News and News Gathering For Television

News, current affairs, features and documentaries represent a sizeable proportion of the total output by the three English channels. The latest BBC report shows that out of a total of 6,438 hours broadcasting in one year, news programmes accounted for 426 hours (or 5·3 per cent) and documentaries and features 1,861 hours or 23·2 per cent. So news and documentaries together account for nearly 30 per cent of the BBC's total television output.

A similar proportion of news and documentary coverage is reported by the independent companies, with news and news magazines occupying as many hours as sport, and news plus documentary output equalling roughly the amount of total time devoted to all plays, series and serials.

News output of ITV

An accurate and impartial news service is required of the commercial companies under the provisions of the Independent Broadcasting Authority Act, and to this end one of the earliest moves by the IBA was to set up Independent Television News. ITN provides a service of national and international news for the whole ITV network, and news is the only area of programming where the supply of material is derived from a single source.

But of equal importance at the local level are the regional news rooms of the programme companies, which provide news and news magazines for their own areas (such as Thames's *Today* programme) and in addition feed local stories of national importance to ITN.

ITN provides over six hours a week of network broadcast

programmes and its principal programme is of course *News at Ten*, the half-hour programme broadcast every weeknight at 10.00 pm. 1974 was the seventh year of *News at Ten*, and the programme regularly reaches the 'top ten' in the ratings, and attracts an audience of some 14 million nightly. The programme uses a successful formula eventually copied by the BBC for its own 9.00 pm bulletin, of using two presenters from a regular cast of five or six (Andrew Gardner, Reginald Bosanquet, Leonard Parkin, Sandy Gall and Gordon Honeycombe) with constant reference to filmed reports, graphics and visuals throughout the thirty minute programme. *News at Ten* is extended to forty-five minutes or longer if the day's news justify lengthier treatment than normal.

On Saturday and Sunday evenings, the main late evening bulletins are curtailed to ten and fifteen minutes, due to the normal lack of news events over the weekend. Every day, there is an early evening bulletin, and on weekdays this is usually at 5.50 pm.

From Monday to Friday, the Independent Companies have recently introduced a lunchtime news programme, *First Report*, which goes out at 1.00 pm, and is chaired by the avuncular Robert Kee, and in his occasional absence by Peter Snow. This lunchtime bulletin is again cut short, with a five-minute bulletin inserted at the beginning of *World of Sport* on Saturdays, and two summaries at the beginning and end of *Weekend World*, when this is broadcast on Sundays.

The regional news rooms of the various contractors devote the major part of their efforts to the various evening magazine programmes which follow the news, at 6.00 pm, coinciding with BBC's round Britain hook-up *Nationwide*. The magazines are broadcast each weekday evening from studios in London, Birmingham, Manchester, Leeds, Glasgow, Edinburgh, Cardiff, Belfast, Southampton, Newcastle, Bristol, Norwich, Plymouth, Aberdeen, Carlisle, Dover and St Helier. The regional news rooms sometimes have other news programmes of their own, like Channel's five minute lunchtime headlines, and their late night news and weather forecast, put out in French.

The pattern of localized news broadcasts can best be understood by a look at the programmes broadcast by Tyne Tees Television in the north-east of England. Their daily weekday

70

magazine is *Today at Six*, which takes an in-depth look at local stories and also shows programmes specially made for the half hour spot on visits to neighbouring foreign countries.

Political stories have their own specialist news programme *Front Page Debate*, which is broadcast on Friday evenings, when local MPs (returned to their constituencies for the week-end) have their say in the studio and are questioned by members of the public. Because the north-east is an agricultural area as well as being the location of several major industries, *Farming Outlook* is an important weekly half-hour programme. Industrial employment opportunities are publicized in *Where the Jobs Are*, a sort of labour exchange of the air, while *Police Call* deals with local crime. With two major football clubs in their catchment area – Sunderland and Newcastle United – *Sportstime* looks weekly at the local sporting scene.

In 1973, Tyne Tees initiated their *Access* programme, as a further extension of their localized news coverage, enabling local groups to put their own case to the public. Issues so far covered have included an examination of the re-development plans for the centre of Newcastle and the importance of the countryside for weekend ramblers. Two Tyne Tees programmes are also occasionally networked – *Face the Press* and *Challenge* – both of which look at national rather than purely local issues.

As London television viewers will appreciate, Tyne Tees covers a well-defined, closer knit area than the 14,000,000 population covered by the two companies in the capital. Thames has done a good job with its *Today* programme, that looks at local issues, with a strong accent on social/housing/travel problems, but London lacks a regional sports programme, in spite of having a dozen football clubs within its catchment area. Nor are Members of Parliament seen very often discussing purely London issues as they do on Tyne Tees.

ITN's *First Report* was launched in October 1970 and currently attracts some 3 million viewers. Because it is not easy to gather news in time for the 1.00 pm broadcast time, the accent is on studio presentation, with spokesmen and commentators brought into the studio, and the occasional use of an on the spot report live, from, for example, outside the TUC headquarters or in Downing Street.

The aim of *First Report* is to cover events that have occurred since breakfast time and the arrival of the morning papers. The production team differs from that producing the evening bulletins (already working a twelve-hour day a lot of the time) and is headed by a producer, with a news editor, chief sub-editor, copy taster and secretary. Five journalists write the news and arrange for the studio guests.

The programme also has its own specialized outdoor broadcast equipment, consisting of a specially equipped Range Rover, with two hand-held cameras, and is especially useful for broadcasting live street interviews.

First Report is extended at the time of the major political conferences, and during the 1973 Labour and Conservative Conferences the whole team and Robert Kee moved to Blackpool and reported from the conference hall.

ITN's evening news programmes emanate from the editorial room at ITN House in Wells Street. There are home and foreign desks, production assistants and typists, assignments desk (who brief the camera crews), scriptwriters and reporters, five film cutting rooms, and separate suites for political, diplomatic, industrial, economic and science correspondents.

Because of the compactness of the set-up, not unlike a newspaper office, camera crews and reporters can be despatched within minutes to outside broadcast assignments. Film is sent back by despatch riders for processing, and often material received after the start of *News at Ten* can be broadcast before the end of the programme.

The 5.50 pm news programme is short and aims to report factually and visually the very latest news. *News at Ten* being broadcast four hours later (and one hour after the BBC's main news programme) allows for greater in-depth coverage, with extensive filmed or taped inserts by specialist correspondents, both home and abroad.

The job of the news programmes is to *report* what is happening and unlike newspapers ITN does not express any political or other opinions. Comment on world affairs is consigned to the current affairs programmes, which are put out by individual companies, although often networked.

ITN is often quicker off the mark than the BBC, whose news coverage tends to be slightly more thorough (e.g. more resident overseas correspondents, etc). During the October 1973

Middle East War, for example, ITN had a camera crew at London Airport within a couple of hours of the declaration of hostilities, and the first film of the fighting on the Golan and Negev battle fronts was beamed to London by satellite within twenty-four hours – *three days* ahead of the BBC. The ITN newsfilm earned an additional bonus by being bought for use in nearly eighty countries. No slouches, the Israelis themselves picked up TV newscasts emanating from Damascus in their Jerusalem studios and were able to syndicate the Syrian coverage of the city under siege throughout the world.

Current affairs on ITV

The selection and presentation of news, whether by a daily newspaper or a television or radio programme, are necessarily conditioned by the twenty-four hour cycle between publication or broadcast. That is, editors show a preference for stories that begin and end in the twenty-four hour period – an assassination, a statement in Parliament, an aeroplane crash, the birth of quads, and so on. The result is that yesterday's news is quite different from today's and tomorrow's.

Looking into the background behind the news, presenting long running stories and comments thereon – a lengthy drought in Asia, progress of the Channel Tunnel, an enquiry into football violence – are consigned to the weekly and monthly publications, and in television to the current affairs and comment programmes. Note, however, that in the case of the examples quoted above, the signing of the Channel Tunnel treaty or the announcement of the results of the football enquiry (events that begin and end within the twenty-four hour cycle) would be subjects for daily newspapers and television news bulletins. To get a balanced picture, therefore, the student of current affairs must read a number of weekly or monthly periodicals, and study weekly television programmes.

'If the job of the news service is to *report* what is happening at any given time,' states the Guide to ITV, 'then the function of current affairs programming is to help viewers *understand* what is happening. And it has to do this by covering situations which may have persisted over weeks, months or even years, and which lie behind and give rise to the events that daily make

73

the headlines. Such programmes, then, will often not take as their point of departure what is immediately in the day's news; on the other hand, since current affairs programmes aim to explain and give context and background to what is happening, they cannot and should not ignore the topical. The effectiveness of current affairs journalism is subject to two major limitations: first, the reporting team's ability to perceive the whole of the given situation, and secondly its ability to bring home in any lasting way to the audience what it is really trying to say.'

The independent companies between them present three major current affairs programmes weekly, which are usually shown in all areas. They are *This Week* (from Thames in London), *World in Action* (Granada) and *Weekend World* (from London Weekend Television). The first two are each thirty minutes long and broadcast on week nights, during prime time, while *Weekend World*, launched in September 1972 following the de-restriction of broadcasting hours, goes out around noon on Sundays, though with a long (some would say, too long) break during the summer months.

This Week tends to specialize in political and social themes, both at home and abroad, and even within these limits its brief is pretty wide. Major programmes included during 1973 featured interviews with the Prime Minister, other ministers, trade union affairs, Northern Ireland. Overseas coverage included Watergate and Vietnam, the drought in West Africa and a look at the current situation in Czechoslovakia.

World in Action was born in 1963 and its style and content in many ways typify the philosophy and lifestyle of Granada Television and its socialist peer owner, Lord Bernstein. Again its brief is global, with a tendency to unearth stories in the manner of, say, the *Sunday Times* Insight team. Their scoops have included an interview with the leader of the Scientologists, Ron Hubbard; Mick Jagger facing a panel of journalists and churchmen; the funeral of Jan Pallach in Prague; as well as thousands of feet of film on the war in south-east Asia; the Guinea guerillas; and industrial and political subjects at home. Their report on the Grosvenor Square anti-Vietnam demonstration won a Cannes award for outstanding television, and there have been others of a similar high standard since then.

Weekend World, hosted by journalist Peter Jay, is in many ways like a serious Sunday newspaper, and normally content is limited to the events of the past week. The programme achieved even greater importance during the 1974 elections, the miners' go-slow, the energy crisis. *Weekend World* suffers from being broadcast late on Sunday morning, when in spite of de-restriction of television hours the British public is simply not yet used to the idea of television viewing. Consequently it reaches a small audience, and in turn attracts little attention from advertisers. Sadly, the programme also suffers from a lengthy shut-down during the summer months, when presumably the programme chiefs argue that news stops happening. All this should be viewed in the light of London Weekend's grandiose promises when applying for the capital's television franchise of a major weekend current affairs programme and the unceremonious disbanding of the public affairs unit within months of going on the air. In case the reader thinks that this is an unwarranted criticism of independent television, it must be pointed out that with the two BBC channels the viewer in search of serious current affairs programmes fares no better with the Corporation, and it has always puzzled me why broadcasters appear to reason that at the weekends our minds go to sleep. The publishers of Sunday newspapers, ever increasing in size with supplements and colour magazines, fortunately appear to think otherwise.

A new arrival during 1974–75 was Thames Television's *People and Politics*, an hour-long programme in which Llew Gardiner interviewed prominent government and opposition personalities. One of his most memorable performances was his quizzing of the hapless Willie Whitelaw on the eve of the Tory leadership ballot. The programme is put out late, usually around 11.00 pm.

Granada's *What the Papers Say* can just about be included here as a current affairs programme. The aim of this breathless twenty or so minutes is to present a profile of how newspapers have been tackling the events of the last few days, using head-lines and quotes. Unfortunately the result is often disappointing, as presenters (who are newspaper editors themselves) struggle to show how clever they are and try to score points off their rivals. The programme is usually broadcast so late, often after midnight, that one wonders who in fact stays up to watch. Its importance equals that of, say, the *Epilogue*.

Other regular and occasional ITV programmes touch upon social and political themes, and these include the regional 6.00 pm magazine type programmes. Other documentary series include Yorkshire's *Alan Whicker*, presented by that excellent reporter of the same name, with his off-beat style and genuine interest in *people*. ATV in 1973 broadcast a series called *Foreign Eye*, hosted by William Davis of *Punch* and the *Financial Times*, which had groups of foreign journalists commenting on aspects of Britain as seen through their eyes. And *very* occasionally, *Russell Harty Plus* and *David Frost* (both London Weekend offerings) deal with social questions, though regrettably these programmes are more often platforms for showbusiness luminaries.

News on BBC television

The BBC, of course, have been in the news business for over half a century, and many more years than their rivals at ITN. Pure news alone occupies some $5\frac{1}{2}$ hours daily of total BBC broadcasting time, including radio, and both television channels and ITV are up against considerable competition from BBC radio – and more recently from London Broadcasting and other commercial stations. The BBC national radio network alone has around a dozen news and news magazine programmes, which include *Today, The World at One, PM Reports, News Desk, The World Tonight, The World this Weekend, Analysis, It's Your Line, Saturday Briefing, Today in Parliament, The Week in Westminster, From Our Own Correspondent, In Britain Now* and several others. And as we have seen, in London, LBC provides an almost continuous news and comment service (some of the latter, though, not of earth-shattering importance), and BBC radio puts out half-hourly summaries on 1 and 2, and hourly bulletins on 4.

Additionally, Television News is broadcast four times daily on BBC 1 and twice on BBC 2, and the pattern is similar to that of Independent Television: an early evening broadcast at 5.45 pm and the main bulletin at 9.00 pm. BBC 1 also broadcasts a lunch-time bulletin, and there are early and late evening summaries on BBC 2.

To provide such a comprehensive news service, the BBC mounts a twenty-four hour operation 365 days of the year, based on the General News Service at Broadcasting House. Television news is located at Wood Lane and television current affairs at Lime Grove, Shepherds Bush. The Corporation also maintains a number of correspondents abroad, rather than relying on agencies or 'stringers' (part-time newsmen), and there are regional news rooms which feed information to the central unit.

Television and Radio News each have their own editors and staff, with radio scoring in terms of immediacy and television concentrating on visual presentation of the news. Some of the major radio news programmes have developed an informal, personal style, such as *Today*, *The World at One* and *PM*, the last two being dominated by the personality of veteran broadcaster William Hardcastle.

The main television comment and current affairs programmes are *Panorama*, *Nationwide*, *Midweek*, and there are other more specialized programmes (*Europa*, for example, or *Money at Work*, which concentrate on specific areas of coverage).

The BBC is probably richer in personnel resources than ITV, and can afford the luxury of a number of specialist correspondents – including the Political Editor and his staff, diplomatic correspondents, and specialists in air and defence, economics, court, industry and labour, science, agriculture and the church. This élite group are equivalent to the highly paid feature writers of the prestige national newspapers.

Overseas correspondents are shifted around according to the amount of news coming or expected to come from a particular area. At the end of 1973, for example, the chief United States correspondent was moved to Brussels to strengthen the EEC reporting team. Recently a correspondent has been sent to Tokyo to cover full time.

Current affairs on BBC television

The main current affairs broadcasts are *Panorama*, broadcast for one hour weekly on Mondays; *Midweek*, of varying length and broadcast on Tuesday, Wednesday and Thursday evenings, and which took over from *Twenty Four Hours* in September 1973. *Talk-In* is a Friday evening series, based in the studio, and conducted by Robin Day and David Dimbleby.

Panorama concentrates on major domestic and foreign topics, and the format allows for studio interviews (Prime Minster, Leader of the Opposition) and filmed reports, which have recently included Bangladesh, Vietnam, the Middle East, and more domestic topics such as pensioners and immigrants. In contrast, *Midweek* is more topical, dealing in depth with news stories – Ulster, European elections, the Middle East war, the energy crisis. *Midweek* was also responsible for the introduction of television phone-in programmes, by which listeners put their questions to panels of 'experts' on the subjects under discussion.

Day and Dimbleby present a nice contrast on Friday's *Talk-In*. Cast rather in the mould of the late Gilbert Harding, Robin Day has a reputation, more or less justified, for rubbing up his guests the wrong way, deliberately or unintentionally, and his behaviour leads to a number of public put-downs by politicians or comments in the press. He still gets an impressive line-up for the programme, and recent guests have included Harold Wilson, Senator Edward Kennedy and Lord Rothschild. The youthful Dimbleby's subjects have included such subjects as student grants and free contraception, though he does, of course, conduct serious interviews with the top names in government.

Nationwide is the BBC's early evening (6.00 pm) magazine programme, which links the regions together in a manner reminiscent of pre-Queen's speech efforts of radio when we really did feel like one big happy family. Coverage is varied in content (everything from sports to rising prices) and ranges over most domestic issues, with no attempt to tackle world events.

The other series programmes, such as *Money at Work* which covers wages and prices, taxation, the stock market, oil, and land ownership, are more specialized. In addition, there are occasional series and one-off documentaries. Included in the former group are *One Day in the Life*, which observes one man and his world for a day; *The Philpott File* (filmed reports from all over the world by Trevor Philpott); and *Yesterday's Witness*, films of past events seen through the eyes of people who participated in them.

Some memorable one-off programmes have included John Betjeman's *Metroland* (a look at suburbia) and *The Block*, about people who live below the poverty line.

Politics and television

Since 1928, the BBC has been free to broadcast on controversial matters though it was not until as late as 1956 that such regulations as the 'fourteen day rule' were abolished, which had prevented radio and television discussion of topics brought up in Parliament until fourteen days had elapsed.

Early general elections, such as that of 1931, were marked by disagreements between the political parties and the broadcasters about how much time should be allotted to them, and it was in 1935 that the Ullswater Committee, reviewing the first ten years of broadcasting, reaffirmed the Corporation's rights to political broadcasting, and recommended closer liaison between the main parties and the BBC.

In 1947 the foundations for the present system were laid. An agreement was reached between the Government, the Opposition and the BBC (recorded in an *Aide Memoire*) and appended to the Report of the Broadcasting Committee of 1949. The arrangements were subjected to some minor alterations in 1969, but the agreement is substantially the same.

The television service is thus left free to arrange talks and discussions on various political topics, but certain programmes are set aside for the use of party spokesmen, and these are agreed between the parties once the BBC has allocated the amount of broadcasting time. These broadcasts are then known as 'party political broadcasts'. Subjects and speakers are chosen by the parties and the broadcasts may be used to reply to the broadcasts of other parties. Since 1965, the Scottish and Welsh national parties have been allocated time in Scotland and Wales respectively. The broadcasts are carried by the BBC and ITV simultaneously. For the calendar year 1972, the arrangements were as follows:

Conservatives – 2 broadcasts of 15 minutes each; 3 broadcasts of 10 minutes each;

Labour – 2 broadcasts of 15 minutes each; 3 broadcasts of ten minutes each.

Liberal – 1 broadcast of 15 minutes and one of 5 minutes;

The Scottish National Party had one five-minute broadcast in Scotland and the Welsh Party one of five-minutes in Wales.

The agreement with the parties also includes a category of broadcasts known as Ministerial Broadcasts, for which the initiative comes from the Government and in which the speaker is a Minister of the Crown. They fall into two categories: the first relate to broadcasts outlining legislation and policies approved by Parliament and seeking the co-operation of the public where there is a general consensus of opinion. To these the Opposition do not have the right of reply.

The second category includes those broadcasts used by the Prime Minister or another senior minister to broadcast information on events of prime national or international importance, and to these the Opposition has an unconditional right of reply. If this right is exercised, then this gives rise to a third broadcast, in which the Liberals can take part in a discussion with representatives from the other two main parties.

Deciding whether a particular broadcast falls into the first or the second category (with right of reply) is a matter that the politicians sort out between themselves.

The Budget also produces two further ministerial broadcasts, one by the Chancellor and a reply by his Shadow, on two successive evenings.

A general election calls for special arrangements and these have been agreed beforehand between the major parties. In 1970, the pattern was as follows:

Labour Party – 5 broadcasts of 10 minutes each;

Conservatives – 5 broadcasts of 10 minutes each;

Liberals – 3 broadcasts of 10 minutes each;

Scottish Nationalists – 1 broadcast of 5 minutes in Scotland only;

Welsh Nationalists – 1 broadcast of 5 minutes (Wales).

In the spring 1974 election, because the minor parties fielded more candidates, the Scottish and Welsh Nationalists and also the Communist Party appeared on national television. The requirement is to have nominated fifty candidates or more.

The broadcasts outlined above apply to television only, and

further party political, ministerial and election broadcasts are also carried on sound radio.

Coverage of a general election of course does not end there, and in February 1974 both BBC and ITV mounted extensive election programmes, culminating in an all-night studio session that dragged into the following day as Mr Heath hung on to the tenancy of 10 Downing Street, and in fact it was not until the Monday following the (Thursday) election that coverage really came to an end.

1964 is generally regarded as the first 'television election campaign', largely because of Harold Wilson's astute use of the medium, timing his evening speeches so precisely that the most important policy statements coincided with the live coverage for the evening television bulletins. (Some commentators reported that his sudden switch to his prepared TV material occasionally left his audience grasping for the thread of his speech.)

Ten years later, we saw the morning marathon party press conferences, held – by agreement – one after the other, with the Liberals winning first prize for innovation: Jeremy Thorpe spoke via closed television link from his Taunton campaign headquarters to the National Liberal Club in London. Again some commentators argued that, like the politicians' 'walk-abouts', the morning press conferences were mounted purely for the purposes of television. Terry Coleman wrote in *The Guardian* (12 February 1974):

'Neither great truths nor even little bits of news emerge from such press conferences. That is not the intention. The intention is to let the television cameras obtain some footage of the leaders which can be used in that evening's news bulletins and the leaders, knowing this, say only commonplace, leader-like things.'

Both BBC and ITV mounted extensive evening coverage of the February election during the three weeks run-up and, should you have so fancied, it was possible to watch at least three hours of politics a night, starting with the BBC 1 extended news bulletin at 9.00 pm, switching to ITV at 10.00 for another hour, and then rejoining the BBC (on its second channel) around eleven.

'In a week-long warm-up for the election,' wrote Clive James in the *Observer* (3 March 1974), 'Robin Day had a good try at injecting the proceedings with some no-nonsense brutality. He was so no-nonsense he was nonsensical and so brutal he was funny. "Would you vote for higher taxation?" he barked at a Liberal candidate, drowning the answer with *"Would you vote for higher taxation?"* and felling the deafened victim with a mighty *"WOULD YOU VOTE FOR HIGHER TAXATION?"*.'

On the Night itself, James continues, 'Robin was merely one among several in a studio full of characters. The best reason for watching more of the BBC's election coverage than of the ITN version was simply that the Beeb's team were eccentrics one and all, and could thereby add to the immediacy of the news the toothsome roundness of their personalities. Robert Kee is nowhere near kooky enough to be a true Election Night linkman. The only ITV talking head who could possibly do the job was to be found doing it for the BBC: a wise theft. Alistair Burnett is Cliff Michelmore's ideal successor – not so well endowed, perhaps, with crass bonhomie but easily his predecessor's equal in patronising snorts and chuckles.'

The extensive coverage afforded the February election worried some commentators, and when the whole event was repeated in October, considerably less television coverage was broadcast. ITN's *News at Ten* was extended to forty minutes, instead of fifty as in February, for example, and although the broadcasters argue that interest was maintained, the viewing public were, I suspect, showing signs of weariness with the whole electoral process, and increasing disenchantment with politicians.

Participation in broadcasts by parliamentary candidates is governed by the Representation of the People Act, 1949 and as amended in 1969. Formerly expenses involved in participation had to be included in electoral expenses but, like the press, broadcasting has been exempt since 1969. However, candidates are still subject to certain restrictions, but in practice the new act has not inhibited straight political reporting.

Televising Parliament

In spite of their willingness – and some would argue their unseemly haste – to appear on all manner of radio and television programmes, politicians are curiously reluctant to allow broadcast cameras inside Parliament. Back in 1966, a Select Committee suggestion to try to experiment with closed circuit radio and television was defeated by a majority of one in a free vote. An experiment was tried, however, in February 1968, starting with the House of Lords and, in April and May, in the Commons, the former using closed circuit television, and the second sound radio, relayed to points around Westminster and edited and played back to Peers, Members and the press. Neither experiment was followed up.

In July 1971, the BBC declared itself ready to carry live on radio the important debates on the question of Britain's entry into the EEC, but the Commons Services Committee voted six to four against recommending this to the House. And in October 1972, the Commons again debated the question of broadcasting proceedings, suggesting further experiments: but the motion was defeated by 191 votes to 165. In February 1975 the subject came up for debate again in the House of Commons, and after a lengthy session members voted for another limited experiment with sound radio only, to be conducted by the BBC and Independent Radio News.

There the matter rests, but as in April 1974 the Government announced the setting up of a major enquiry into broadcasting headed by Lord Annan, presumably this is one of the areas that will in due course be investigated and reported on.

Meanwhile, Britain will remain the only country in Europe that does not allow the broadcasters into the parliament. Worldwide, twenty-one countries allow some kind of television broadcasts of parliamentary proceedings, and a further twenty-nine have radio coverage. In West Germany, for example, parliamentary debates are regularly reported, and total annual output of direct television is some sixty hours. The French allow occasional televising of debates, as do the Italians. The nearest we have come to it in Britain are the experiments listed above, and the only programme broadcast to the public has been the early 1974 experiments by BBC Radio London with meetings of the Greater London Council. But if Britain appears to be dragging her feet perhaps we should recall that it was only just over two centuries ago (in 1771) that newspaper reporters were allowed inside the Mother of Parliaments.

To sum up the position of broadcasting and politics, some statistics for the year 1972–73 might be appropriate: during this twelve-month period, some 667 appearances were recorded by Members of Parliament on BBC television (2,131 in network radio programmes). These involved some 259 MPs in television and 364 on radio – some of them appearing more than once. And since the 1970 Election, the BBC calculated that 370 MPs had appeared in television programmes, and 486 on radio.

What is interesting is the comparatively small number of Members who appear regularly on television. These obviously include Ministers and others holding key positions in sensitive areas (such as William Whitelaw in Northern Ireland, and his successors), and the Prime Minister and Leader of the Opposition. But television once it has used someone for a broadcast and found them satisfactory tends to go back for more: this phenomenon applies more to the BBC, I feel, and also works in other areas, such as television drama, which accounts for the feeling that we continually see the same faces appear on television: we are right, we do.

Some Members of Parliament and other public figures have in a way played the media men at their own game: they co-operate by timing their public announcements to suit the media, and lunchtime is a good time – catching the evening papers and television bulletins – and even go so far as to issue texts of their speeches in advance. This results in newscasters coming out with lines like 'In a speech to the members of the Dorking Ladies Guild being given about now, Labour MP Mr . . . says that . . .' Where speeches have been reported in advance of their being given, newspapers particularly have occasionally been caught out, as for example when a speaker failed to turn up at a Guildhall banquet and what he 'said' appeared in the following day's press.

As a public relations exercise, the techniques used by certain public figures are admirable. Duncan Sandys had an efficient secretariat and his pronouncements were often controversial and invariably well timed. Enoch Powell, no less well organized, can always be relied upon to say something worth quoting. For a time at least, such public figures become television *performers* – remember Jimmy Reid and Upper Clyde Shipbuilders or 'Big Lil' who led the Grimsby trawlermen's wives back in 197?.

Because television (and the other media) are constantly seeking out *human interest* angles, there is bound to be a concentration on personalities, and this tendency may obscure the real news and encourage biased reporting. How this affects the news we see – or don't see – will be examined further at the end of this chapter.

Eurovision and other broadcasting groups

In the gathering of news available for broadcasting, the European Broadcasting Union and other agencies and groupings of broadcasters play an important role, and both the BBC and the IBA belong to a number of these. The European Broadcasting Union, of which the BBC's Director General, Charles Curran, is President, is an association of broadcasters, with thirty-three active members in Europe, and some sixty-three associate members in other parts of the world. The EBU was born in 1950, following a conference convened by the BBC and held in Torquay to discuss co-operation between broadcasters, particularly on the question of news programmes. The result was the creation of the Eurovision link, by which the constituent members 'offer' their available news coverage (a football riot in Italy, a train crash in France, an election in Germany) to the other members on a daily basis. If members agree to take coverage, having viewed what is offered over a closed circuit television link, then a hook-up is arranged.

Eurovision works with other broadcast groupings, such as Intervision, which performs a similar function inside the communist bloc, and with American broadcasting organizations, so that coverage of world events by satellite can be arranged by means of a block booking, the cost of which is shared among the participating members.

Eurovision has its headquarters in Geneva and a technical centre in Brussels (for many years inside the roof of the Palais de Justice because good reception could be achieved there), and in the course of a year some fifty thousand television news items are offered on the programme exchange, and over five hundred sports programmes. The BBC is Eurovision's largest contributor, and the smaller the country or broadcasting organization (Switzerland, Austria) the more coverage they will take from Eurovision, to minimize the cost of news gathering.

Because of the disparate nature of its membership, which includes governments with every shade of political opinion, some censorship by members is inevitable. Spain and Portugal, for example, may not like to offer news coverage of strikes or riots, and under De Gaulle the French were touchy about similar areas of news. When this occurs, the BBC or ITN may fly out their own camera team (and subsequently offer their coverage to other Eurovision members) or one of the other agencies – Visnews, UPITN – may arrange coverage.

The main function of Eurovision is the exchange of news items, but its creation has led to the birth of a number of peculiarly European programmes, most famous of these being the annual *Eurovision Song Contest*, held in 1974 in Brighton, and *Jeux sans Frontières* (*It's a Knockout*), which gives an annual lift to sagging summer viewing figures. These international programmes rely on high visual content to overcome the barriers of language.

In 1974, the EBU's twenty-fifth annual general assembly was held in England. The BBC and IBA are regular members of its councils and various sub-committees (technical, legal, liaison, etc.).

The Corporation and the Independent Companies are also associated with other international groups – the Asian Broadcasting Union, and the Commonwealth Broadcasting Conference, among them. This latter group has a permanent secretariat housed inside BBC premises in London and the 1974 conference in Cyprus was preceded by a meeting of the standing committee in London.

The BBC were strongly represented at the second World Conference of Broadcasting Organizations held in Rio de Janeiro in 1973 and are represented on committees of the International Telecommunications Union (the broadcasting arm of the United Nations), the International Radio Consultative Committee (CCIR) and the International Telegraph and Telephone Consultative Committee (CCITT).

Comparisons with France and America

News coverage under General De Gaulle was frequently the

subject of government censorship – 'television is government in the living room,' one minister commented. Invariably news bulletins started with an item showing the General's activities for that day and in the face of a hostile press, De Gaulle more or less took over the ORTF for purposes of propaganda.

These manipulations inevitably led to a revolt by journalists during the events of May 1968, when nearly all of them resigned. Since De Gaulle's fall from power there have been slow improvements but, as in other areas of broadcasting, the service remains technically brilliant but frequently lacking in imagination. For example, one observes coverage of a fire in a department store accompanied by a superimposed musical sound track (to add excitement to the drama?) so that, apart from the absence of jerky, stop-frame movements by the participants, the result is not unlike an early Mack Sennett comedy film.

The effect of tight control over broadcasting has meant that a lot of younger, creative producers have abandoned the languishing television service in favour of French cinema. This accounted for the bureaucratic, production-line appearance of much of the ORTF's output, with the added result that in a country surrounded by rival broadcasters (Europe 1, Andorra, Monte Carlo, etc.) a large percentage of the population tunes in to programmes from *outside* the country.

The ORTF was further shaken by the *scandale* of 1972 when producers were accused of taking bribes to discreetly plug certain products (e.g. by showing shots of, say, an airline) – most of them publicized by the state-owned advertising agency, Havas. Although the *affaire ORTF* led to a parliamentary enquiry, it did not result in any significant relaxation of censorship under President Pompidou. Even if it were possible to introduce freedom of speech on television, as one producer remarked, with the proliferation of political parties in France this could lead to disaster.

News broadcasting in America is largely in the hands of the three major networks – ABC, CBS and NBC – with early evening bulletins stretching from 6.00 until 7.30 pm each evening: sometimes they start earlier, as in Los Angeles for example, regarded as the most news crazy city in America. There is no editorializing as such, though local stations frequently broadcast an 'editorial', which is announced as such, at the end of the news bulletin, and invite comment and a reply. These can concern local or national affairs and many differing points of view are aired.

The news features I viewed were often concerned with social issues: I remember an excellent three-parter dealing with the latest craze for the Chinese martial arts and pointing out the dangers to young children.

Actuality coverage is generous and British viewers of the Watergate hearings will have appreciated that the events being recorded often provided more drama than most of the fictionalized serials. When the networks get their teeth into a story or a scandal, they rarely let go: witness *The Selling of the Pentagon*, a CBS programme that attacked the way the government had 'sold' its Vietnam war policy, and criticized by Vice-President Agnew, of all people, as being 'un-American'. These documentaries and comment programmes unfortunately stand out like oases in a desert of consumer-oriented television, with the result that serious-minded Americans look to the press as their major source of news coverage.

Some comments and conclusions

There is no doubt in the minds of broadcasters that television reporting has contributed to the public's greater awareness of the world.

'I see our job here,' said Philip Whitehead of *This Week*, 'in this particular programme as getting very sophisticated political information on a number of different levels through to an audience of people who habitually read the *Daily Mirror* and who are not, because of education or interest, capable of going through all the better alternative sources of information.'

Television journalists, because by the very nature of their profession they believe in freedom of speech, feel that their role as educators and communicators is an important one, and frequently come into conflict with the notion that television is purely showbiz and should be geared to the ratings. Not that serious commentators despise the ratings: they want their programmes to reach the widest possible audience, but a line has to be drawn, with the effect that items are not slotted into a current affairs programme for no other reason than it will attract more viewers without them.

But even with genuinely lofty ideals such as this, it is hard for serious broadcasters not to be hamstrung by the very nature of television. For years sound radio was the source of authoritative news and in the early days of television, right up, in fact, to the creation of *News at Ten*, television news was little more than an extension of radio. When news pictures were introduced, they were copies of cinema newsreel techniques.

This emphasis on the visual tends to colour the choice of news coverage, with the effect that a certain amount of censorship exists by virtue of the process of selection or rejection of items by news editors. Why, then, do we see so many films of motorway crashes, with their undoubted visual impact, when the event affects relatively few of us, beyond the occupants of the vehicles involved and their families and friends? This is not to argue, of course, that road accidents should not be high-lighted in the news, as a warning to other motorists. My argument is that the visual impact of an event such as a road accident tends to push out information on, say, new government social policies. And if the broadcasters see their role as one of educating a population that on the whole does not read serious newspapers, then non-visual items of news must surely receive more prominence.

This process of selection and rejection *within* individual programmes has a wider counterpart when broadcasters have to decide whether a news or documentary programme itself should be included in the schedule or not. 'The Press' includes everything from the *Mirror* to the *Financial Times*, and the reader takes his choice: but to put on a documentary about the energy crisis may mean postponing or cancelling Tom Jones, and if television is geared to money, Tom Jones will inevitably win.

In Britain at least, thankfully, television executives have always given fair regard to their obligations to 'inform and educate' and in the patterns of broadcasting outlined in preceding chapters we have noted that as total broadcasting hours have increased, the *proportion* of time allotted to serious broadcasting has remained fairly constant: if there is more sport, there is also more news. It is curious in the light of this that both the BBC and the IBA when putting forward their claims for the fourth channel should suggest that *this* is the one that would be used for more serious broadcasting. It certainly has not happened with BBC 2.

This consideration raises two points: should television be regarded fundamentally as no more than home movies, a permanent source of on-tap entertainment, with no more right to try to influence our lives than a theatre play or variety show? Most broadcasters would argue that television has a duty beyond that of providing continuous distraction. Given this, and to come to my second point, television must get away from the necessity of providing more and more news and documentaries simply because there is more and more time to fill.

A useful parallel might again be taken from publishing, where many small independent firms work happily alongside giants who turn out several hundred books a year. I questioned an editor who had moved from such a large firm to set up on his own and he explained the reason why. 'I was in charge of a department that had to produce thirty books a year. I asked what happened if one year I said I could only find twenty books that I, as editor, thought were worth publishing. Ah, my bosses replied, we must have thirty books, because our overheads are costed on this number, the salesmen have to be kept occupied, the warehouse kept stocked, the printing presses working. So in the end I was producing books for no other reason than they were required to keep the business at a certain economic level.'

While television people are always complaining about lack of funds, particularly for serious programmes, one cannot but criticize the amount of wasteful duplication that is apparent, through the policy of regionalization. In this area, the IBA is probably the worse offender, and it is only by close examination of their annual report or by leafing through the pages of the fifteen regional editions of *TV Times*, that one realizes that there is a wealth of programme material available that one will simply not see, because it is broadcast only inside a limited area. Even if you accept television's duty to feature localized issues, I cannot see that a programme on, say, Africa should only be seen in Scotland, simply because it was made by the television company there.

The television companies also show a reluctance to buy in

documentary material from outside. This is particularly distressing at a time when concomitant with a general decline in the British feature film industry (largely through the withdrawal of American money) there is a resurgence of interest in the documentary and short film generally. But like the author who wants his books to be read, the short film maker complains there is no outlet for his work. The arguments given by the television companies are that the unions will not allow outside material, anyway, we can make a film about this subject ourselves. O.K., why don't they? The very essence of a documentary is personal involvement in the subject being covered – the film must have a point of view. Surely the more talent that can be crammed into television the healthier the industry would be.

No amount of television hardware will make up for absence of talent – or lack of opportunities for talent to reveal itself. This is the tragedy of, for example, American television, where the studios and equipment are the finest and the personnel among the most expert, but the medium is hamstrung because of the demands of the advertisers. It was only the creation of the public service channel that opened up opportunities for freelances to exhibit their wares and television is the richer for it.

Finally, I come to some considerations of the content of news and documentaries as we now see them. Arguments are constantly raging about whether television reflects life or, in fact, helps create a lifestyle, and nowhere is the distinction more blurred than in news coverage.

Any producer or cameraman will tell you that people act differently when they are on television (in spite of what the BBC may argue about their weekly saga of *The Family*) and, going a stage further, the presence of television cameras may even *provoke* certain actions. Which then came first – the act or the reporting of it by television? Take, for example, the Trafalgar Square rallies, or the frequent protests about pedestrian crossings, where we are treated to the sight of yet another crocodile of suburban mums wheeling prams and blocking traffic on a major trunk route. Without television coverage, these manifestations would probably never have happened, and by being televised their importance is magnified out of all proportion to their significance.

This blowing-up of minor events has another interesting side effect in that, because all television news is news, we tend to view atrocities in Vietnam with the same detachment as the results of a Miss World contest. Which brings me back to my point about using news items simply to fill available television time. I have often wondered, for example, if the day will come when ITN will announce that tonight *News at Ten* will be cut to twenty minutes instead of thirty for no other reason than there is a lack of worthwhile news.

Reducing all events to a common denominator has an effect on people as well, which all professional broadcasters should bear constantly in mind. Because television can create instant personalities (and destroy them, as in the case of, say, Simon Dee) we tend to endow the pronouncements of a Cabinet Minister with the same authority as the protests of a Camden squatter or even the claims of a washing powder salesman.

Television, finally, distorts. Television presents issues in a visual, ephemeral way, so that issues that are complex are presented as stark black and white. Life, as we all know, is simply not like that.

Events can be stage-managed for television purposes. Perhaps the most horrifying example of this is the incident of the television crew who held up the shooting of a condemned man by firing squad for thirty minutes while they set up their cameras. Even interviews can be prepared in advance, with questions and answers being rehearsed. What is more insidious, perhaps, is the increasing use of television by public figures to make important pronouncements: former Prime Minister Heath used this method, and now every minor politician or trade union leader is goaded on by reporters to throw out a challenge to the other side or pronounce on the kerbside whether such and such an offer is acceptable or not. Gradually, delicate negotiating situations are being taken out of the meeting room and on to the screens because of television.

Inevitably the process of selection and rejection – using whatever criteria (visual impact, topicality, news value) – must lead to a certain amount of bias. Television, both BBC and ITV, has been variously accused of favouring or attacking Conservative, Labour and Liberal, while in America President Nixon concentrated most of his attack on the media on the area of television, as did former Vice-President Spiro Agnew.

And we have already noted how France's De Gaulle tried to use the television news as a means of personal propaganda.

While these extreme situations are comparatively rare, because of the independent mindedness of newsmen, some unconscious bias still creeps in: American television films South Vietnamese war atrocities but neglects to cover the Vietcong; French reporters decry racial conflict in South Africa but do not report on ethnic problems in Paris or Marseilles.

The only safeguard would seem to be to apply a policy of rigid separation between news coverage and documentaries; between fact and opinion.

Finally, just how great an influence is television presentation of news and documentaries? In a recent survey of television, *Newsweek* magazine put forward the neatly opposing views of British broadcaster Ludovic Kennedy, and of Olivier Todd, senior editor of the French magazine *Nouvel Observateur*. Kennedy plays down the influence of television, particularly its ability to sell us *ideas* and argues that at best it helps to reinforce existing ideas and prejudices: Labour supporters will watch and applaud a Labour party political broadcast but will deride Edward Heath. Todd, by contrast, points to the success of Liberal leader Jeremy Thorpe in the 1974 February Election: Thorpe's television appearances sold him to the mass of British voters, while Edward Heath and Harold Wilson suffered from a degree of over-exposure. Todd goes on to expand his theory of three types of television coverage – 'ghetto' television, where control is in the hands of a power élite; 'saturation' television where in the interests of fairness and objectivity everyone has an equal say and cancels each other out; and finally the 'low calorie' system, where the opposition is given as little exposure as possible.

Hopefully, if we are to believe Kennedy, 'the human mind, like the human body, has a habit of rejecting what is foreign to it, that people everywhere will think what they want to think, whatever anyone "on the box" may say.'

5. Sport on Television

Sports coverage on BBC and ITV accounts for a substantial amount of broadcast hours, roughly the same as the amount devoted to current affairs and documentaries or bought-in feature films, around ten hours a week. This amount of coverage is dramatically increased to cope with major sporting events, at which the BBC in particular excel, such as Wimbledon fortnight, the Olympics and successive World Cups.

Sports broadcasts account, then, for between 10 and 15 per cent of all television output – 772 hours in one year on BBC 1 plus a further 287 on BBC 2, making a grand total of 1,059 hours. Expressed as percentages, this represented 15·6 per cent of total broadcast hours on BBC 1 and 9·3 per cent of BBC 2 or 13·2 per cent of the total output of both channels. After current affairs, features and documentaries (annual total of 1,861 hours or 23·2 per cent of output), sport is the next largest group of broadcasts, and twice as much coverage is accorded to it as to children's programmes or drama or light entertainment. And those who feel that there is too much 'religion' on BBC television will doubtless be surprised to note that religious programmes account for 1·8 per cent of broadcast output, or one-sixth of the time devoted to sport.

Historical background

Our awareness of the amount of sports coverage on television probably dates back to 1966, when the World Cup series was played in England in July and August of that year. It was this event 'that changed the BBC's reasonable approach to sport to an obsession,' in the words of Milton Shulman (in *The Least Worst Television in the World* – see Bibliography for details),

94

and it is true that it was the success – unexpected in some quarters – of the BBC's blanket coverage of the World Cup that led also to a re-think by ITV some two years later.

Let us first look at the BBC's position. During the 1966 World Cup, the schedules of BBC 1 and 2 were revamped to accommodate live and recorded coverage of the games and, as England progressed towards the Wembley final (which they won), viewing figures rose, during what are normally two bad months for television statistics. Encouraged by this success, the BBC decided to apply the same blanket coverage to the Mexico Olympics in 1968 (over 200 hours of broadcasts), the Mexico World Cup in 1970 (with, to quote Shulman again, 31 hours of football in the week of the general election that returned the Conservatives to Westminster), and the 1973 Olympics from Munich. And early in 1974 they announced plans for extensive coverage of the World Cup, to be played in West Germany, although England exited from the competition almost a year previously.

All this sports coverage was in addition to the regular screenings of League and Cup football programmes, racing, tennis, athletics and a host of minor sports that included show jumping and table tennis.

With the advantages of possessing two channels and one central administration, the BBC inevitably scores when it is a question of covering the big event. Split up into a mass of regional companies, the IBA is in a weaker bargaining position and has virtually given up the fight to compete with the Corporation in certain areas. This does not mean that the independent companies bow out of all the major events: on the contrary, many of these, such as the FA Cup Final at Wembley, are covered live simultaneously by both BBC and ITV. But any initiatives to cut down on this wasteful duplication are more likely to come from the IBA than the BBC, who refuse to consider alternative coverage of such major events.

ITV has, however, improved its sports coverage since 1968, as the result of consultations held since the 1966 World Cup series, and coincidental with the appointment of London Weekend Television as the London contractor. London Weekend is now responsible for the Saturday afternoon sports' presentation, which runs from around 12.30 until 5.00 pm when the final results are given, and which is broadcast under the general title of *World of Sport*, in direct competition with BBC's *Grandstand*.

World of Sport is introduced from the LWT studios by Dickie Davies, who is supported by a number of sports administrators behind him: Bill Ward, chairman of ITV's sports committee (and a director of ATV); John Bromley, Deputy Controller of Programmes (Sport) for London Weekend; and Gerry Lofthouse, who has the tricky job of network negotiator.

ITV's re-shuffle was, I suspect, a move designed to counter some of the domination of Saturday afternoons by the BBC. By introducing wrestling at around four o'clock – and one might question the inclusion of this undignified spectacle in a legitimate sports programme – the ITV cleverly engineered a massive switch-over from the BBC to their channel to coincide with the start of wrestling. The BBC have not really fought back against this, and their sports coverage simply continues with racing, cricket, rugby or show-jumping coverage, while BBC 2 runs an old movie for the people who protest about too much sports coverage on television.

The pattern of ITV's Saturday afternoon coverage then looks something like this:

12.45   Introduction by Dickie Davies from the studio. 'On the Ball' football preview by Brian Moore
 1.30   The ITV Seven (formerly 'They're Off'), with racing coverage from two or more meetings
 3.00   An international sporting event, e.g. cycling
 3.55   Half-time football results, reports, news
 4.00   Wrestling
 4.45   Full round-up and results service

BBC TV adopt very much the same sort of pattern, starting with a football round-up by Frank Bough and Sam Leitch, the latter sitting impassively in the studio and lacking a lot of the feeling of involvement of Brian Moore. Cricket, racing, show jumping, rugby then follow, according to the season, and final scores are given at 4.45, parallel with ITV. As can be seen, the bulk of sports coverage centres around horse racing and football, and later on Saturday evening the BBC have recorded highlights from one or more matches (lasting about an hour) and ITV reply with the 'Big Match' on Sunday afternoon – recorded highlights from their main game, with goal sequences and shorter spots from two others. Both channels run viewers' competitions, such as 'Penalty Prize' or 'Golden Goals', testing knowledge of football events.

In midweek, ITV and BBC offer coverage of football and other sports events, depending on important League or Cup fixtures at home, or clubs' involvement in European soccer competitions. Boxing and athletics are also covered, though the BBC seem to have a preference for these while ITV remains firmly football oriented. BBC's weekday coverage currently centres round newcomer Tony Gubba, who acts as studio linkman.

During 1972–73, BBC 2 tried its hand at sport, with a Thursday evening feature programme hosted by writer/actor Colin Welland and Ian Wooldridge, a sports writer with the *Daily Mail*. Because Thursday is traditionally football's night off, live coverage of games was obviously out, and the programme attempted to get behind the scenes of football and other sports, but the attempts were marred particularly by Welland's subjective approach to the programme. He insisted, for example, on being filmed training with his favourite club, Leeds United, and his participation in the programme, instead of letting the players speak for themselves, reminded me of BBC's *Blue Peter*. The programme was not continued.

Football on television

The amount of football seen on television is governed by the rivalry between the two competing channels and by their complicated agreements with the Football Association and the Football League – the former association being the controlling body of the sport in England, in charge of all 'leagues' of which the Football League, embracing the ninety-two professional clubs, is the most important member.

Periodically there are arguments between the football authorities and the television companies, with demands for more money for match coverage and anguished cries from the broadcasters, and at best there is an uneasy truce operating between the two sides. At the time of writing, the television companies have been paying about £1 million for three season's coverage of Saturday Football League matches, and in a series of meetings held during 1973 the companies offered an increase of around 40 per cent on this figure, which the football authorities considered too little.

The BBC/ITV offer (and the only time they come together is when they need to present a united front to the football administrators) was based on a payment of £240,000 each per season, worked out at a rate of some £4,000 per match covered, two a week, for thirty weeks of the year. In addition a disturbance allowance would be paid to the club visited: this sum varies from £50 to £250 and is little more than a token payment.

This agreement covers only League matches and separate agreements would have to be negotiated with the League and the Football Association for screening competition matches (League Cup, FA Cup, etc.) and with individual clubs who might be involved in European competitions such as the UEFA Cup (where the fees are retained by the club). Additional income is gained from the sale of advertising banners around the pitch. There is a tacit agreement that these are allowed by the TV companies where they are permanently fixed in position, though there has been some astute changing of copy by agencies a few days before the televising of an important game and it is known that the cameras will inevitably pick up the banner. Where this involves European games relayed over the Eurovision link the value to the advertiser can be considerable.

The agreement with the League does not mean that the television cameras have automatic right of entry to the clubs of their choice for the screening of football matches. There are agreements with the League about dipping into the lower divisions several times each season (an attempt to present a balanced view or a device to scare off viewers?) and in the case of the BBC the programme has to be screened after 10.00 pm (on Saturday evening). Individual clubs may also refuse to allow cameras on to their grounds: in the past these have included Burnley, whose chairman Bob Lord has consistently opposed televising of football, Notts County, Everton and Fulham. The arguments against coverage are various, but generally club directors fear that it will adversely affect their gates.

The costs of covering matches do not end with the fee paid to the FA and the League (whatever that will eventually be), and estimates put the cost of mounting coverage at around £18,000 to £20,000 per game. And as we have seen, only portions of games may be transmitted, so that two halves of one game do not make up a programme, when dealing with League fixtures.

ITV have additional problems of networking, as matches to be televised are selected several weeks (eight to ten) in advance, and the ITV negotiator has the job of providing a balance between the various programme companies. The BBC and ITV alternate in first choice of available games, and the BBC are looking basically only for two a week. ITV then have to juggle between companies (for Granada will want to cover the Manchester and Liverpool clubs, for example) and rival commentators. Occasionally a compromise is worked out, with two commentators covering, say, Arsenal v. Manchester United, for London Weekend and Granada respectively.

The pattern of television coverage can be gained by a look at the programme for January 1974:

Filmed extracts shown for the first time were:

Football League	13 matches	3 hrs 19 mins.
FA Cup Rounds	18 matches	5 hrs 36 mins.
Football League Cup	2 matches	1 hr

The total out of 33 matches (or 50 hours of football played) was nine hours, 55 minutes. In addition, library material and news totalled 2 hours 20 minutes during the period under review. The above figures do not include the other parts of the programmes – comment, analysis, discussion – but the amount of time football was shown on the screen.

The usual argument against football coverage on television is that it adversely affects attendances at grounds. *I can, however, find no evidence whatever to support this view.* Because of this fear, the television companies cannot advertise in advance which games they are screening, but even in a small town (e.g. Ipswich, Bristol) where the arrival of television vans on the Friday could hardly be disguised, there is no evidence that gates

99

fall as a result. On the contrary, commentators regularly report packed grounds and frequently capacity crowds for the matches they are covering.

Additionally, it should be borne in mind that transmission of the matches covered is after the event, when the results are known, and this way corresponds to the reviews printed in the evening and Sunday papers. The companies realize that a lot of the excitement is lost if the result of a match is known, and when broadcasting results often deliberately omit the score line of a match about to be screened (though they will cheerfully use news bulletins as a means of showing filmed highlights of a match the rival channel is broadcasting).

Because match coverage is bound to be something of an anticlimax, the programmes have developed into analyses of play, comment and discussion, and, above all, have led to the cult of football chat-show personalities.

Football's chat artists

It probably started with television coverage of cup finals, when in an attempt to grab viewers the companies started transmitting their pre-match warm-up earlier and earlier in the day, so that now it begins soon after breakfast on the fateful Saturday in question. This means designing a programme of filler material – recorded highlights from previous rounds, interviews with the participants and their managers, and above all the introduction of a panel of experts.

Although this phenomenon is apparent in other sports, including rugby, it is in football that they are supreme. Invariably, they include players (Jack Charlton, Paddy Crerand, Bob McNab) and managers of successful – and not-so-successful – clubs (Don Revie, Bill Shankly, Malcolm Allison, Brian Clough).

The result has been, some would argue, that the personalities have started to overshadow the game, so that Clough's problems with Derby County and his eventual move to Brighton rated as much press coverage as George Best's frequent resignations from football and his brushes with a former Miss World. The fact that any of these events should have made news at all

is questionable, and it is paradoxical that footballers rarely manage to leave the sports pages unless they are divorced or in some sort of trouble.

The personality cult was carried to an extreme during the live coverage of England's disastrous game against Poland in October 1973 (which cost England their place in the World Cup), when ITV's panel, scarcely held in order by the urbane Brian Moore, and consisting of Clough, Jack Charlton, Allison and Derek Dougan, could hardly contain their emotions at England's defeat and Sir Alf Ramsey's management. This sort of display, worsened by Clough's attempting to suggest that he was somehow involved in England's performance, may make for lively television but tended to overshadow the point of the programme: that England had lost a vital match.

By contrast, BBC's coverage of the game, with Jimmy Hill (a recent capture from ITV), Don Revie and Bobby Charlton, was an example of sober analysis, with the participants refraining from scoring points off each other for public display.

It is always difficult to make a dull match look interesting and problems arise when what promises to be an exciting clash ends in a goal-less draw. By the time the result is known, the best the programme company can do is edit out the worst bits and emphasize the highlights. This can lead to overuse of the 'action replay' (a favourite habit of the BBC) during the game and afterwards in the analysis. It also means that programmes may have to be padded out with interview material. This is not often successful, as players are not necessarily articulate people, and rarely look ahead beyond next Saturday's game, so that a worthwhile comment or two is dragged out to a full five minutes of unpromising question and answer.

At one time the football authorities criticized the attention paid by the cameras to fouls and fist fights, and for a while the cameras retreated. Thanks, however, to increasingly imaginative direction, with the impetus coming from ITV, this convention was quietly ignored and the cameras now get in amongst the action. Distasteful as fouls and brawls are to observe, in the hands of experienced commentators such as Hill and Moore – who have consistently condemned unfair play – they give a deeper insight into football which is suffering more every

101

season from gamesmanship and 'professional' tactics such as tripping, time wasting and shirt pulling.

As a commentator on some of the more serious aspects of the game Jimmy Hill is without rival. A former player, chairman of the players' union and successful manager of Coventry City, Hill is fearless and authoritative, unafraid to speak his mind on such topics as the handling of Frank O'Farrell by the Manchester United directors at the height of the George Best affair in December 1972. Television as a whole chooses to glamorize footballers and I would personally like to see more time given over to some of the more worrying aspects of the game – physical and mental stress suffered by players, the high failure rate among apprentices and lack of provision for the future. This fault is, of course, not common to television alone, as Britain lacks a serious, adult sports publication that will concern itself with these wider issues, and both the sports pages of the nationals and the specialized football magazines appear to be catering for a basically juvenile readership.

The cult of sports personalities, being a totally artificial business anyway, has meant that certain names have come to the fore, to the detriment of other, equally well-informed manager/commentators who rarely get a look-in, so that it is hard to recall the last occasion when Liverpool's Bill Shankly – one of football's most consistently successful managers – was last featured in an in-depth interview.

At commentator level, Brian Moore (ITV) is good, though he tends to get a little over-excited, which one might find jarring. Huw Johns (ITV, Midlands) is kindly, paternal and you get the impression that he cares about the 'lads' playing out there. Best known of the BBC commentators are Barry Davies who transferred from ITV and who does a workmanlike job, and David Coleman, whose position has been somewhat over-shadowed with the arrival of Jimmy Hill.

The FA Cup Final is – World Cups apart – the biggest event in the television soccer calendar. Here, as mentioned, the companies are starting earlier in the morning with each succeeding year and rivalry between the two channels is intense. In 1973, ITV boasted a higher camera tower so the BBC promptly hired a helicopter so that they could go one better. In an earlier year, ITV pipped their rivals by having commentators clad in tracksuits to interview managers and anyone else they could get a microphone to in order to record their minute by minute impressions of the game.

All this could well go by the board, if at any time the football authorities and the television companies fail to agree on financial terms for coverage. If this should happen, presumably television can turn to European and world soccer – and feel free to screen it at 3.00 pm on a Saturday afternoon!

Horse racing on television

Television's other major obsession, after football, is with horses, either over the sticks or on the flat, and it is in this area, as other observers (notably Milton Shulman) have demonstrated, that television must bear a moral responsibility for the unprecedented spread of gambling in Britain, into an industry that sustains 14,800 betting shops and risks some £1,500 million annually in bets, four-fifths of this amount on horses.

Both the BBC and ITV encourage betting, either directly or indirectly, linked with their coverage of certain races, notably the *ITV Seven*, and bookmakers refer to these combinations in their advertisements. The programmes compound the harm done by announcing the results of what you would have won if you had followed the experts' guidance – but without announcing whether anyone has actually won (except on rare occasions when an elated viewer telephones to announce his good fortune).

Clearly, to my mind, gambling is not sport and these programmes do little more than encourage the commercial exploitation of gambling. By occupying so much television time, little coverage is as a result accorded to athletics, swimming, gymnastics, tennis (apart from the Wimbledon bonanza), cycling and many other sports, where programmes that encouraged *participation* by involvement and imitation, could widen interest in activities other than the placing of bets on horses.

This is not to suggest that minority sports do not receive attention on television: some do, to a point where they are eventually publicized out of all proportion to their following or in many case their entertainment value. This has been the case

103

with the BBC's passion for show jumping with the result that we know more about 'Doublet' than about many an athlete's performance in the Olympics. Judging from the membership of riding clubs in Britain, it is doubtful if more than 100,000 people actively participate in the sport. Yet one regional sports centre, Crystal Palace, alone is frequented by more than 450,000 active sportsmen in a year. So what about badminton, basket-ball, billiards, bowls, boxing, canoeing, cricket, cycling, fencing, gymnastics, hockey, judo, netball, polo, rowing, sailing, skating, skiing, squash, swimming, table tennis, weightlifting?

Regional sport

It is again outside the capital that television manages to get involved at grass roots level with local sport. HTV produces *Sports Arena*, Ulster has *Sportscast*, Yorkshire screens *Yorksports* and *Sportstime* appears on Tyne Tees Television. These programmes concentrate on local sporting events and personalities.

Encouragement to participate in sports activities is confined to adult education, where Granada have covered angling, table tennis and snooker, Thames have featured boating, and Yorkshire riding, tennis and golf.

A noteworthy contribution in this area was BBC's *Sportstown* which featured competitions in various sports between youth centres in different towns. This is more constructive than coverage of many of the so-called minority sports which have included everything from snooker and arm wrestling to stock cars and polo.

6. Religion on the Box: the God Slot

Televised religion excites so many passionate arguments, both for and against, that it is as well to examine the amount and type of coverage accorded to it by the BBC and ITV in the light of accurate figures – if such are available – about worship and church-going in Britain, in much the same way as one might consider the need for greater coverage of fishing on television in relation to the number of anglers.

There have been a number of excellent reports on television and the place of religion therein (see Appendix I and the Bibliography) and I shall be referring to these continually in my text. Mention should also be made of the vociferous religious pressure groups – Festival of Light, Lord's Day Observance, Mary Whitehouse *et al.* – who tend to emit rather more heat than light, and who tend to cloud the real issues and create an impression of more substantial support that I feel they in fact warrant.

Let us take a look first at the strength of religious adherence in Britain.

The churches in Britain

The Church of England is the established church in England, and derives this status from the Reformation. The Sovereign must always be a member of the Church and major ecclesiastical appointments are made by her and the Church must obtain Parliament's consent to changes in its form of worship, as contained in the Book of Common Prayer. The Church is (highly) organized into 43 dioceses, split into two provinces of Canterbury (29) and York (14). The dioceses are subdivided into parishes, of which there are 14,250 – or roughly the same number as there are betting shops. Official statistics claim that

105

of the 46 million people resident within the two provinces, 60 per cent are baptized into the Church and some 20 per cent confirmed.

The General Synod – the Church's central administrative body – is responsible, among other things, for the provision of a number of schools in England and Wales, which are attended by 11 per cent of the 8·6 million pupils at publicly maintained schools. The Church is an independently wealthy body; its assets in land and investments amount to some £434 million, and its annual income is £27·5 million (1971–72) – and rising.

Other major religious groups include the Church of Scotland, with 2,070 churches; the Methodists, with just over 600,000 members; Baptists with 250,000 members. Other Free Churches include several minority groups such as the United Free Church of Scotland, and other Protestant denominations embrace such diverse sub-groupings as the Churches of Christ, the Quakers (a mere 20,000 members) and the Salvation Army (350,000), Mormons (100,000) and Christian Scientists (300 branches).

The Catholics are more accurate at counting heads and claim 5·5 million adherents and among the Jewish community 400 synagogues cater for 410,000 Jews.

It is not surprising perhaps that religious broadcasting put out by both BBC and the IBA (according to a 1970 IBA survey) appears to reach nearly two-thirds of the population, with just over half the viewers polled claiming that they took note of religious programmes. It is horrifying to note that Yorkshire TV's *Stars on Sunday* has claimed audiences of 12 to 15 million people, and it is appropriate that we should now look at the sort of output beamed at the so-called religious audience.

Religious programming

Both the BBC and the IBA spend a considerable amount of time, personnel and money on the production of religious programmes, which account for some 3 per cent of total BBC output (including radio), or two to three hours a week on television and nine to ten hours on Radios 2 and 4. ITV puts out some two or three hours of religious programming at weekends, plus other (regional) programmes such as Thames's *Epilogue* during the week.

During 1972–73 BBC Television broadcast a total of 128

hours of religion on BBC 1 (2·6 per cent) and 16 hours on BBC 2.

Among the Independent Companies, religious output was only marginally less than home-produced drama (i.e. excluding imported films, series and serials), or children's programmes, or education programmes.

The responsibility for BBC religious programmes rests with the Religious Broadcasting Department, which serves both radio and television, and boasts a staff of forty, with an equal number of secretaries and assistants. There are also the Roman Catholic Assistant and six regional broadcasting organizers, and a host of advisory bodies which we shall examine later.

The BBC spends about £2 million a year on religious broadcasting, of which about £1·6 million goes to television. Figures are not available from the IBA, because of its constituent members, but in addition to a nucleus of IBA headquarters staff concerned with religious programmes, some fifty part-time advisers are retained by the various companies, and producers of other types of programme also work on religious programmes. Jess Yates, who produced *Stars on Sunday*, has – not surprisingly – worked in television variety.

Ever since the concept of the Reithian Sunday, with its religious services and solemn music, dating from the early twenties, the idea that the Sabbath should be the main time for religious broadcasting has firmly taken root. For those interested, the two main blocks of religious output are on Sunday mornings, usually featuring a 'morning service' type of broadcast, and the evening closed period from 6.15 to 7.25 (known irreverently in the trade as 'the God Slot') which features discussions, Bible quizzes and, invariably, hymn singing. What then is the object of all this religious output?

The BBC has defined its attitude thus (and here I quote the Church of England Broadcasting Commission Report (see Appendix I below)):

'The first aim is that it should reflect the worship, thought and action of those churches which represent the mainstream of the Christian tradition in the country. The second is that religious broadcasting should bring before listeners and viewers what is most significance in the relationship between the Christian faith and the modern world. The third aim is that religious

107

broadcasting should seek to reach those on the fringe of the organized life of the Church or quite outside it.'

The IBA claim that they are broadly in sympathy with these aims, though its more recent policy appears to have been one of 'let's look at all religions, including for example those coming from the East and which are so attractive to the young,' and this exercise is conducted with the same uninvolved expertise that one would apply to an examination of rock formations or the lives of Hebridean crofters. 'While five years ago the push was all towards a social gospel, now there is a fresh readiness to share spiritual things,' says the IBA yearbook.

I criticize both definitions for their extreme vagueness and, like politicians, churchmen are not good at defending their positions when put on the spot. What, for example, is meant by 'the Christian tradition' or 'the organized life of the Church' (Sunday school, the annual nativity play, vicars' tea parties?). This same woolliness appears in the Church's report when it goes on to examine the various target audiences for religious programmes and speak of aims such as: 'To bring men and women to (deeper) commitment to Christ in the fellowship of His Church' or 'to relate the Faith to the daily realities of life, to provide a Christian philosophy.'

Even members of the Commission, which gave rise to the Report quoted above, were not always happy with television's religious output. Certain discussion programmes were attacked for their 'tragic lack of Christian content' or 'too great a predominance of the discussion-and-debate element over proclamation and teaching' (i.e. hammer it home and don't let's argue?), as a result of ever widening interpretations of what was religious broadcasting. In fact, one programme – Granada's *Seven Days* – was almost indistinguishable from any current affairs or documentary screening, and London Weekend were refused permission by the IBA to show an interview series during the closed period because of its lack of 'religious content'.

In an attempt to clarify the Church's differing views about the purposes of religious broadcasting, The Rev. Michael Saward (at the time the Church Assembly's Radio and Television Officer) attempted to define the three possible views as follows:

'(1) Religion equals life. The sacred and secular are regarded as being co-terminous. According to this view, every programme is religious if it "evokes a religious response".

'(2) Religion is the relationship between God and the individual soul. The sacred and secular are set in opposition to each other. This view sees broadcast religion primarily in terms of direct evangelism.

'(3) Religion is the relationship between God and the Soul worked out in every aspect of life. The sacred and secular are related but not co-terminous. This view seeks to bring the supernatural to bear upon the whole range of human concern.'

In an earlier speech, the then Archbishop of Canterbury had urged an even wider breadth of approach, saying that 'religious television should depict human problems just as they are, human situations just as they are, arouse interest in them as human situations and then see what the Christian faith can do with those situations in a practical way.'

The broad and narrow views have led to some polarization of attitudes among both churchmen and broadcasters, dividing themselves into those who favour a soft sell ('all television is religion') and the hard sell, with the emphasis on proselytizing. As the Report goes on to state that, 'It is a fact that conversions can and do take place through the medium of broadcasting' (although no evidence is adduced in support), perhaps one could argue a case for apportioning time to the various religious blocs in much the same way as for party political broadcasts, and viewers should be warned in advance about what to expect.

Religious output on BBC

What then, in the light of arguments between churchmen and broadcasters, is the type of religious programming that actually results?

The casual observer of BBC (and indeed ITV) religious programmes will invariably get an impression (correct) that output consists of church services, hymn singing and a certain amount of earnest discussion. The services are served up under the guise of *Family Worhip* or *Morning Service* or some other title, and are spread, apparently evenly, between the major competing religious denominations. The broadcasts are always live and not recorded, the argument being that the service broadcast should be the one being conducted on that particular day, and the Catholic church in particular is touchy about its complicated liturgy which is closely linked to the sacred calendar.

Because church services are not *exciting* events, the director and cameraman are restricted in their treatment: long shots of rows of old ladies in their best hats, or close-ups of angelic choirboys or nurses or Salvation Army girls produced as it were out of a hat, particularly at Christmas time. Another diversion is the architecture or stained glass especially if it is an old church. The services usually end with the 'blessing' after which we are presumably to depart feeling suitably uplifted.

Hymn singing is also a staple of the evening religious period currently under the guise of *Songs of Praise*. Unfortunately the articulation is so bad that it is usually not possible to understand the words being mouthed by the performers, and captions are sometimes used for the viewer's enlightenment. The hymns are interspersed with short introductory bits pronounced by an earnest BBC man who would be just as much at home on *Come Dancing* or *Top of the Form*.

Religious chat shows take all sort of forms, from examinations of social problems (praiseworthy) to interviewing eminent figures (Dame Flora Robson, for example) and trying to elicit from them their ideas about 'religion' or 'Christianity'.

Religious quizzes, based upon knowledge of the bible, have as little relevance to religion as questions on Greek mythology or some of the obscurer moments on *University Challenge*. I have observed several of these programmes set in garish, ecclesiastical surroundings (i.e. the quiz master's desk looks like a jazzed-up pulpit) and feel that the likely result is to turn the uncommitted sharply away from organized religion.

The ITV effort

Both channels are necessarily ratings conscious, and have to bear in mind that the evening religious slot follows the early evening news and immediately precedes the peak evening viewing slot (in the case of ITV this can be the *Palladium Show*). Choice of religious programming is therefore influenced by these considerations and ITV consequently has been more adventurous, if that is the word, in its use of the God Slot.

Coverage of church services is shared out between the five major network companies, minus Thames (London weekdays), who take the lion's share of the available slots (just over a hundred a year), with ten or fifteen of these awarded to the smaller regional companies. The fixtures are then apportioned between the various religions, in a manner similar to the coverage of football matches.

The major networks also effectively control the evening religious slot, and here some often disastrous experiments have been attempted. Among them must be included London Weekend's *Roundhouse*, a 'religious' debate that bordered on bedlam; Granada's *Seven Days*, already referred to; and ATV's *Beyond Belief*, described by the Church's Report as aptly titled. There are occasional imports, such as *Adam Smith*, the daily life of a parson, who might well have been a dentist or at best a social worker. Tyne Tees Television attempted a series based on telling the gospel in modern form, and starring Cliff Richard, but this failed to reach the networks, for which we should be grateful, in spite of questions in the religious press.

And there is *Stars on Sunday*, probably the most mimicked religious programme ever broadcast. *Stars* was produced by Yorkshire's Jess Yates, who also worked in light entertainment, and Yates also appeared in the show (Robert Dougall then took over) – introducing guest artists who sing comforting songs and reading viewers' letters, with all the slick professionalism of a David Jacobs or Peter West. The number of nationally and internationally-known performers who have been drawn to the programme is amazing, and one can only assume that the money is good and the exposure (to 15 million viewers in the C2 to DE range) is valuable. The settings are cosy – Victorian or farmyard; the choice of songs saccharin sweet and cloying; the introductions sanctimonious and unashamedly directed at the lonely and housebound. One expects Wilfred Pickles to pop up at any moment, to 'give 'em the money'.

As to the programme's religious content, the Church and indeed the IBA have mixed feelings, though the former has supplied endorsement in the shape of the Archbishops of Canterbury and York and the Catholic Cardinal Heenan, who

111

have all appeared on the programme, and indirectly given credibility to the utterances of, say, actor Raymond Burr (*Ironside*) who also appears. This is the reason of course why this sort of programme should be condemned: 'religion' is effectively equated with an establishment, middle-class way of life (solemn music, heavy drapes, voices intoning bible readings), and graphically draws a distinction between 'them' (the pious-looking hymn singers who may well be rapists for all we know) and us, the viewers.

Religion fares a little better outside the acknowledged Sunday closed periods, and Thames television is just one of the regional companies that puts out a nightly *Epilogue* type of programme. These feature more than the 'earnest parson dispensing spiritual bromide' of the Church's Report, and laymen are frequently used. Little expense is allowed on these productions and inevitably by their transmission time – after a bank of commercials – most of us will have switched off.

Religious topics receive the coverage they, on the whole, merit in news and documentary programmes, such as *First Report* or *Good Afternoon* (for women) and in the regional magazine programmes. Socio-religious questions are frequently examined and screened during prime time and these programmes have included recently a look at the work of the Salvation Army, the study of Muslims in Great Britain and the treasures of the Vatican. Perhaps more use could be made here of material gathered – and sometimes filmed – by church people engaged in missionary work in underdeveloped countries overseas, and, given the address of the order or organization concerned, many of us viewers might be inclined to salve our consciences and send off a donation. Appeals, including those for numerous religious and social causes, are of course regularly broadcast on both television and radio, and choice of participants is governed by a complicated selection process, but as these are broadcast during the Sunday evening religious period some viewers must be lost.

(The references to 'lost viewers' and slotting of religious programmes before the start of prime time viewing by television people does seem to imply that they regard viewers as television addicts, who switch on their sets at the start of the evening and cannot be distracted enough to switch to another channel or even switch off. Surely there is also a body of viewers who *select* what they wish to view?)

Religion also crops up in plays and series with non-religious themes (for example, the vicar in Yorkshire's *Emmerdale Farm* regularly puts over Christian ideas in an extremely palatable form) and some series, for example ATV's *Crossroads*, is frequently used to expose social themes, as we shall examine later. There have been several attempts at religious comedy, largely thanks to the efforts of actors Derek Nimmo and Donald Sinden, and clergymen, albeit stereotyped, make their appearances in such series as *My Wife Next Door* and *Oh Brother*.

Religious programmes have spawned a crop of television personalities who are known to be 'concerned' about the 'traditional values'. Usually they are of an upper-class mould – Malcolm Muggeridge, Lord Longford – with the occasional sprinklings of youth (Cliff Richard?) and typical housewife (Mary Whitehouse). Altogether, an uninspiring lot, and watching an enlightened interviewer trying to make headway with these worthy representatives is as depressing as trying to reason with a Jehovah's Witness on your doorstep.

Where non-experts have been introduced into religious programmes they have recently included former boxer/greengrocer Henry Cooper (talking on Southern's *Guideline* epilogue programme about the influence of God in his life) and Sir Alec Douglas Home who appeared in Scottish Television's *Dilemma* series, on a similar theme. Religious phone-ins have also been tried by Barry Westwood, a veteran of religious television, on London Weekend. Southern Television ran a Christmas carol competition and pop star Alan Price has composed contemporary music for Good Friday telebroadcasts. Certainly the television companies cannot be accused of not trying.

Training of the shock troops

The two major churches, Roman Catholics and Protestants, run training centres for use by clergy – and others, such as social workers – to learn how to use television. The Churches Television and Radio Centre at Bushey (C of E) is run by the Rev. Leslie Timmins and permanent staff include Bertram Mycock, who worked in radio in the north of England. The

Catholic Church has its own Radio and Television Centre at Hatch End, Middlesex.

The Bushey Centre started in 1959 (originally based in Tooting, south London) with limited equipment consisting of one camera and a monitor, but thanks to grants from the Lord Rank Foundation for Christian Communication it has expanded to include some of the finest colour television closed circuit equipment, said to be worth some £350,000, housed in a new £200,000 building. Annual running costs are put at £100,000 and the Centre is used by clergy from all denominations from bishops down to curates, and lay people involved in education, social work, etc.

The Catholic Centre is on a more modest scale, and run by Father Agnellus Andrew, who is an experienced religious broadcaster. Equipment is valued at some £80,000 and annual running costs are put at £57,000. Much of the finance needed to run the Centre comes from annual parish church collections and course fees do not cover the costs of running them.

Courses at the centres last for one or more days, usually three or four, and are concentrated into small groups. Professional broadcasters are often used, such as Ivor Mills, a newscaster with ITN.

Religious advisory bodies

Both the BBC and IBA are advised on general religious matters by a number of specialized religious advisory bodies. For the IBA, these include their Central Religious Advisory Committee, which offers guidance on general policy matters, and the Panel of Religious Advisers, who assist with particular programmes or series, with special sub-groups for Scotland. Each programme contractor in turn then appoints religious advisers, who concern themselves with that company's output only. The various groups are broadly representative of the main religious denominations and include both clerical and lay members.

The Central Religious Advisory Committee also advises the BBC and has a membership of twenty-nine. It normally meets twice a year and has separate sessions with the BBC and IBA. The sort of general topics discussed included in recent months an examination and report on religious output, preparation of a paper on Programmes of Worship, and considerations of its own procedural functions. Members usually serve for a term of five years.

Looking at the functions of the CRAC, the Report of the Church's Commission on Broadcasting had three main reservations (in addition to its general disquiet about the influence of the Committee as a whole). First, that the meetings were not sufficiently frequent: it suggested that programme sub-committees meeting more often should be appointed to report back to the full committee. Second, through meeting more often, the sub-committees would have more direct influence on programme planning, particularly in the early stages, before a new programme or series went on the air, and not simply comment after the event; and finally, that regular reports of the proceedings of the committees should be published, so that the churches could be seen to be exercising some influence on religious broadcasting output.

As a step towards greater consultation between the Church of England and the broadcasters, a Standing Conference on Broadcasting was set up in 1973, to provide a forum for discussion between churchmen and producers. For day to day information and guidance, the churches operate some very efficient information services, which include the Church Information Office (Church of England) and the Catholic Enquiry Centre, though the churches complain that their advice is not always sought or, if given, necessarily heeded.

What of the future of religious broadcasting on television? Church sources claim that some five million people are regular church attenders, and if this figure is accepted, it represents ten times the number of people attending, say, football matches. On that basis, coverage of religious matters could be considerably extended.

To be successful in extending the influence of religious programming, it would seem logical to put an end to the Sunday 'closed period', which technically ceased to exist with the de-restriction of broadcasting hours in 1968 and the introduction of normal commercial breaks into the religious slot. The closed period has the effect in many homes of encouraging viewers to switch on just that much later in the evening (around 7.35 in time for the normal evening programmes) and it is questionable whether religion should be protected by having a special segment allotted to it on both channels, so that the element of competition between BBC and ITV is effectively removed.

Allowing religious programmes to compete with drama or current affairs, at no special set time in the evening and in competition with the other channel(s), would surely lead to a raising of production standards and to more imaginative use of the number of hours that traditionally are reserved for religion.

7. Television Drama

Television drama is the only 'theatre' that 90 per cent of the population experience and, as we have seen, right from the earliest days of BBC sound radio, the broadcasting of plays has been an important section of the output of the Corporation. And even pre-war television experiments from the Alexandra Palace studios included two plays a week for the first three years.

Now nearly 6 per cent of BBC 1's output – and nearly 7 per cent of BBC 2 – consists of drama and in the 1972–73 period this accounted for 298 and 213 hours respectively, or a grand total of over 500 hours of televised dramas. This figure of course includes series and serials, and sadly is exceeded by the hours of imported (mainly American) films and series, which accounted for over 1,100 hours on BBC alone.

Perhaps we should note at this point that BBC radio puts out over a thousand hours annually of plays and series, over its four networks.

Since the de-restriction of broadcasting hours, the independent companies have been putting out just under thirty hours a week of television drama, including again series and serials, an area in which they are particularly strong. Unlike the BBC, with its centralized resources and flexibility of programming, ITV suffers from having a network of separate companies, each with its own drama department. In times of ever rising costs of production, this makes for unnecessary duplication and the predominance of the major network companies. And ITV is as always tied to rigid time slots, including commercial breaks which may hamper production.

Overall the output of the three television channels represents the 'largest theatre' in the world – with audiences of ten million or more for a single play not being uncommon – and British television represents the largest TV drama complex in the world. Certainly not a bad record, but how does the product stand up in practice?

The need for writers

One of the recurring themes of this present book has been that in the case of television broadcasting more is not necessarily better, and once again this is unfortunately true of television drama. Whilst it is undoubtedly gratifying to anyone interested in the wider spread of culture among non-theatre goers, because there is so much television drama broadcast it makes demands upon creative resources that cannot necessarily be fulfilled.

All theatre has to be written, and while the ordinary viewer or, more likely, the frustrated playwright, may get the impression that the same writers are used over and over again ('not another Johnny Speight series . . .') television drama producers and directors argue quite forcefully that they are straining all the available talent and they are doubtful if there are in fact any untapped sources of further plays.

Already the novels of the nineteenth, eighteenth and seventeenth centuries have been scoured for drama plots; translations and adaptations are made from every language in the world, from the Greek classics to obscure dissident Russians; and yet there is still a crying shortage of material. The BBC, being the public service that it is, maintains a full-time script unit that reads and assesses thousands of unsolicited manuscripts annually, and publishes a booklet for would-be broadcasting writers, through BBC Publications.

The BBC drama department consists of three major groups, dealing with single plays, series and serials, and each of these is subdivided into a smaller unit, each consisting of, say half a dozen television directors and a dozen producers, with supporting ancillary and secretarial staff. All this does not include the people involved in actually mounting an eventual broadcast of a play – costume, design, construction, casting, electrical, lighting and other departments.

In addition to the script unit itself, within each of the drama groups there is a host of script editors, whose jobs include searching for new writers, dealing with adaptations from published novels or treatments (outline ideas for a play or series), liaison with existing known writers, and doing any work necessary on a submitted and accepted script to bring it to the screen.

On the question of untapped talent, Irene Shubik, for many years director of BBC's *Wednesday Play* series, is adamant. 'Again it may sound arrogant, but I really think I am in a position to know about original talent and there really isn't any. There is no reason why there should be. You could not fill a West End theatre every night of the week with a marvellous new play.'

Mention has already been made of rising costs, and it has to be borne in mind that for every play actually presented on television, many more will have had time and talent spent on them though they may never reach the screen. For a series of, say, thirty plays in a year, loosely linked under some overall title such as the *Wednesday Play* just mentioned, fifty or sixty plays will have been considered and worked on, and thirty of them ultimately rejected for, among other things, reasons of cost (too large a cast, expensive location shooting may be involved, difficulties of finding the right actors and actresses, and so on).

Because so much money is at stake, producers and directors cannot afford or are not allowed to take risks: it costs as much money to mount a play by a successful, known author as by a new, untried one. But one failure can embarrass the whole of a television department or company or even cost the producer his job. So it is safer to fall back on tried and tested writers (and to a regrettable extent on tried and tested formulae, as we have seen when examining American series output).

Indirectly, television is something of a patron of writers, assisting them even when their plays do not get on to the screen, by the work done in the script unit already described. Some of the regional ITV companies also offer writing awards or scholarships to encourage new writers. What is certain is that as television output continues to grow, more and more trained TV writers will be required.

The cost of television drama

Television plays are one of the most expensive forms of entertainment that the BBC and ITV companies are obliged to screen. They cost more than sports presentations or talks and occasionally more than variety – in the latter case the cost is often linked to the salary demanded by the 'star' performer. The cost of mounting a television play will depend upon a number of factors, and these include the cost of acquiring the basic script. This as we have seen may be a published novel, but if it is out of copyright, no fees will normally be payable, but in all cases there is the cost of adaptation and/or translations, and writers have to be hired to do this work. In the film industry the cost of acquiring and developing the property (as the script is called) is usually budgeted at something like 10 per cent of the overall production costs, so for a movie costing several hundred thousand pounds – and that is cheap by Hollywood standards – the script is a not inconsiderable item. All this means that coupled with the general shortage of writing talent, higher fees are paid for film than for television scripts, and the best writers could be lured from the BBC or Granada to Universal or Paramount. Fortunately writers are not only concerned with money (or perhaps this book might not have been written).

Because television drama costs so much to mount, as mentioned in the previous section, there is a danger of relying on established writers and formulae. The independent companies are also tied to the ratings and to justify the high cost of TV drama producers have to present plays that attract large audiences and, therefore, increased advertising revenue. The BBC does not have this problem, but is nonetheless caught up in the ratings battle as a means of periodically asking for an increase in the licence fee.

The tendency, then, must be to present plays in a form that will appeal to the broad mass of the television audience. Fortunately here, again, both writers and directors fight against this and, notably in the case of the BBC and certain of the independent companies (e.g. Granada), are allowed to express themselves and present what kind of plays they want, with little or no regard for the ratings. This does not mean, of course,

120

that all plays have or should have a 'social theme' and as else-where in television, producers try to achieve a balance of output, with a comedy play followed by a serious drama, a modern play being succeeded another week by a classic, and so on.

One of the ways of attracting viewers regularly is by broadcasting television plays in a regular slot, e.g. *Play for Today* or the *Wednesday Play*, or grouping plays together under a theme title, which the independent companies are particularly fond of doing. So in recent years we have had *Questions of Sport* or the *Love Story Series* and *Country Matters* or *Six days of Justice*. These theme groupings should be distinguished from series (e.g. *Napoleon and Love*) where a group of plays are centred around the same central figure, and serials, which are perennial soap operas and include everything from *Coronation Street* to *Emmerdale Farm, Harriet's Back in Town, Marked Personal*, and many others. Theme groupings help to build regular audiences for plays, i.e. viewers know what to expect, and familiarity is one of the most attractive qualities in programming, but can be cramping for writers and other creative people, who are forced to work within the confines of the theme.

We have already mentioned on the question of costs that unlike the BBC, which has the advantage of a centralized drama unit and nationwide broadcast facilities, each of the major network companies in independent television has the problem of mounting its own drama department and competing with other companies for air time on the network. The fate of the smaller regional companies is even more severe. To get a network showing they must produce something pretty original, and for this they have to risk money they cannot really afford to lose if they do not get a showing. Their problems are not unlike those of the independent film maker who may produce an excellent movie but is restricted as to his outlets because of the stranglehold of the major distribution networks.

Linked to the cost element is the problem of the speed with which drama productions have to be got together and broadcast. We have noted that with the advent of telerecording, which originated in America because of the need to cope with the different time zones, drama no longer needed to be produced live, with actors terrified of drying up in front of the cameras. With video recording, the television industry turned its studios

121

into production factories. In America, this has, as in other areas, been carried to an extreme, and studios like Universal in Hollywood, have twenty or more major network series in production at any one time, with a concentration during the summer months ready for the new autumn schedules.

Unfortunately, just as the television moguls were investing money in bigger and better studios, the creative people – writers, directors, cameramen – were starting to move away from the confines of the studio and acquire a taste for documentary drama, using lighter, hand-held film cameras (not videotape) and shooting on location.

The first signs of this came in the early 1960s when some observers argue that television drama reached its zenith. It was during this era that BBC's *Z Cars* first made its appearance, and we saw individual, striking plays such as Tony Garnett's *Cathy Come Home*. This was the start of the innovatory documentary technique, a form that has been used consistently well by such writers as Peter Terson (*The Fishing Party* and other plays).

Conversely, the move away from the studios, while reducing demand for the capital investment needed in land and buildings, can add significantly to staff costs, as film crews are on different pay scales to those working inside television, and overrunning even by a day can bring agonies for the producer, who has to allow extra money for actors and crew at often crippling pay rates.

Drama imports and exports

The bunching of plays into theme groups was described by one world-weary BBC producer as a device forced upon him by BBC Enterprises to enable them to sell part of their output to overseas markets. There may in fact be some truth in this and, as we shall see when we discuss more fully the question of overseas sales and imports into Britain, this is often a useful way of marketing hours of television output in convenient blocks. The Americans particularly cannot think in anything less than terms of thirteen or twenty-six weeks, their major fear being that once they have invested money in building up an audience for a particular series they will promptly lose it again if they cannot follow the thirteen-week block with another, equally powerful, series.

From an artistic point of view, imports and exports present serious problems. For the writer working inside British television, any pressure to Americanize his output is irksome and the results, if he gives in, can be disastrous. Witness for example the dreadful *Avengers* series or *The Persuaders* – if these can rightly be introduced into a discussion on drama – which were products written and cast for an indeterminate mid-Atlantic market, as glossy packages.

Unfortunately the result is that this type of television series loses a lot of its intimacy. Themes can only be touched in a most superficial way. Characterization becomes less subtle, as 'types' have to be established in a form that is truly larger than life, so that every level of audience will be able to recognize the stereotypes being portrayed. Examples of this type of production, usually emanating from the American west coast, are numerous, and they include the stock policeman, doctor, clergyman, hippie, adoring housewife roles, that any television viewer will instantly recognize.

Without the single play you have no series, and without series you have no drama. And it is thanks to the BBC and other far-sighted organizations that the single play is encouraged and writers allowed to blossom.

Drama and commercials

What is increasingly worrying to those who view television purely as a means of making money for the stockholders is that TV drama steadfastly refuses to conform to the television way of life, as portrayed by the commercials. As we shall examine in Chapter 9, commercials present a basically spurious picture of life, where depression is 'lifted' at the drop of a Disprin and the right kind of car will get you the right kind of girl.

Television writers, on the other hand, are concerned with life as it really is, and many of the newer, younger television playwrights are increasingly concerned with social problems and exposing them by means of a serious television play, often of the documentary type.

Is there advertising pressure on drama producers and directors? Most would say not. In Britain at least we seem able to separate output from advertising, in much the same way as the dichotomy is preserved between the editorial and advertising departments of newspapers. ITV suffers from the need to fit plays into slots of thirty, sixty or ninety minutes (slightly less, owing to the air time of the commercials inserted) but argues that the commercial break can in fact be used by the playwright as a device similar to the interval between acts in the theatre, to denote the passage of time or the movement from one location to another. But the rigidity of the time slots can lead to a certain artificiality in cutting or extending plays to fit the minutes allowable. The BBC's policy is much more flexible in this regard, and programmes, often on BBC 2, overrun and bear little resemblance to the times scheduled in *Radio Times*.

Television serials

These are something of a speciality of Independent Television, and two of the longest running are *Coronation Street* (Granada) and ATV's *Crossroads*. Because these two programmes are viewed so frequently it is easy to lose sight of the fact that much of the acting is of an extremely high standard, so that the characters of pub landlady Annie Walker (played by Doris Speed) or motel owner Meg Richardson (Noele Gordon) are so firmly established in the viewer's mind that we tend to *forget that they are only acting*.

Daytime series from the independent companies include Yorkshire's *Emmerdale Farm*, a television version of *The Dales* or *The Archers*; *General Hospital* (ATV); *Crown Court* (Granada), which gives an interesting insight into the working of the courts, with a 'case' being presented over three half-hour periods each week. Other shorter-lived serials have included *Hadleigh* (the story of a country squire), *Van der Valk* (Thames), the saga of an Amsterdam police officer, and various other *policiers* – *Special Branch*, *Hunter's Walk* (slightly more credible).

ITV make a special point of mentioning that serials, which undoubtedly attract massive viewing figures (*Coronation Street* and *Crossroads* appearing regularly in the Top Ten ratings), are deliberately used to put over religious or social points of view. I have already mentioned the frequent appearances of the local vicar in *Emmerdale Farm* where he spoke his views on divorce and christening, among other topics. *Crossroads* is more often used as a vehicle for putting over social questions, and according to ATV these have included such a wide range of subjects as mental health, loneliness, vandalism, religion, local government, pollution, education, abortion, childlessness, illegitimacy, kleptomania, prisons, prostitution, nursing, bigamy, illegal immigrants, teenagers, old age and attitudes to death. One might, of course, wonder by what right television drama producers push so much 'propaganda' at the viewer, but it must be pointed out that discussions are held with doctors, clergy, marriage guidance counsellors, solicitors, social workers, police, prison governors, and many other knowledgeable experts before embarking upon these themes listed. Where traditional religious programmes may be failing, the drama department could be said to be performing a useful, responsible function.

The major BBC serials are both police dramas – *Z Cars* and *Dixon of Dock Green*, both of which manage to retain their feeling of authenticity after many years of screening. Some of their top writers are regularly involved, and each presentation is a complete story, without an underlying threadline, apart from the regular appearance of the police cast. N. J. Crisp, and Alan Prior are just two of the 'name' writers who contribute to these programmes. Another regular programme, popular in some quarters, was *The Brothers*, a story of a family-owned transport business, and among the most popular series must be included the Barlow programmes (*Softly Softly*, *Barlow at Large*) and the *Lotus Eaters*, featuring Ian Hendry.

Single plays and themes

Because the output of all three channels is so large, it is difficult to recall and single out many excellent individual plays. The main BBC slots are *Play for Today* and *Play of the Month*, which present the best usually in modern drama. One producer did point out that their passion for the off-beat had sometimes caused problems as 'viewers now watch *Play for Today* hoping to see something rude'.

Again the very best writers are employed, and memorable recent productions include *The Reporters* (Arthur Hopcraft), *The Bouncing Boy* (John McGrath), *Kisses at Fifty* (Colin Welland), *Speech Day* (Barry Hines) and a memorable play, for me, from an earlier year, *Circle Line*, featuring Michael Feast as the young hippie caught on the never ending round of life. More scope for individuality is given to writers of the *Thirty Minute* plays, and themes have recently included *The Edwardians*, *Six Faces*, and *Sextet* (a series of plays for a repertory of six artists).

On Independent Television, Granada, Yorkshire, ATV and Thames provide the bulk of the single play and theme play output, with London Weekend being conspicuously weak in this area.

It was Granada who brought us *Shabby Tiger*, *Country Matters* and *Sam* (including its later revival), and the excellent adaptation of Stan Barstow's *Raging Calm*. *Love Story* came from ATV and was excellent, while Thames offered *Napoleon and Love*. *Armchair Theatre* is one of the network's major slots during the week, and it is unfortunate that London Weekend do not offer viewers more serious drama over the weekend period. However they did come up with *Helen, A Woman of Today* (by the writer of *A Man of Our Time* which starred George Cole some years previously), *Intimate Strangers* and the occasional excellent single play, among which I would list a favourite of mine *Achilles Heel*, about the problems of a professional footballer, and featuring Martin Shaw.

One ITV disaster should not pass without mention – *Divorce His: Divorce Hers* starring the Burtons, which came from Harlech, one of their rare appearances on the network. And another (from London Weekend) series that was hated by the critics was *The Aweful Mr Goodall* (usually described as 'awful' without the 'e'), though Robert Urquhart who played Goodall did his best with some unpromising material.

A lot of what the television companies would classify as light entertainment can usefully be examined under the heading of drama, particularly when dealing with situation comedy series. One of the features of the 1974–75 period was the apparent lack of fresh comedy material on our screens, and the welcome re-appearance of the BBC series *Whatever Happened to the Likely Lads*, which includes some of the finest drama script writing ever broadcast. Another repeat series featured Ronnie Barker in *Porridge*, a funny/sad look at prison life.

Sad to observe was the general rise in the level of violence portrayed in drama series, notably *Special Branch* amd *The Sweeney*, both from Thames Television, and *The Hanged Man*, a series about a building boss who dodges numerous attempts on his life. Violence was all too common in the numerous imported series from America, including *Kojak*, *Ironside*, *Macmillan and Wife*, and many others with a recurrent cops 'n robbers theme. That the BBC should spend public money importing much of this rubbish is indeed little short of scandalous.

8. Children's and Educational Television

If you mention children's television or education on TV to the average viewer, there is no doubt that he would conjure up a jumble of pictures that included such programmes as *Jackanory* or *Magic Roundabout* or *Blue Peter* through to afternoon presentations designed for school term-time viewing or the dully presented talks by earnest professors put out under the aegis of the Open University. In a way, he would not be far wrong, and in this section we take a comprehensive look first of all at children's programmes and then examine how television is fulfilling its function as educator.

The BBC

Being the vast and complex organization that it is, the BBC devotes considerable man-hours, energies and talents in the fields of children's and educational programmes, both on radio and television. Children's programmes on BBC 1 account for nearly 10 per cent of output on that channel, that is, considerably more than for drama (6 per cent) or news (4·7 per cent), while programmes classified as 'schools' take an additional 7·6 per cent of BBC 1 air time and further education 4·7 per cent. All told, then, over a fifth of BBC 1's output is concerned with education and children. The decline in the use of radio for schools is reflected in the low percentage of output on Radios 1 to 4 devoted to children's and schools programmes (about 4·5 per cent of output).

Educational broadcasting started fifty years ago (with BBC radio) and although radio output has been severely curtailed and more time given over to television, the BBC itself reports that some 33,000 schools make use of schools radio programmes against only 28,000 having television sets. This latter figure represents about 85 per cent of total schools.

In theory, radio and television programmes for schools are designed to be complementary and not competitive, so that the best use is made of resources. As a result, most language programmes will be broadcast on radio, while geography or science subjects, relying on greater visual content, are best presented on television. (I would query in passing why this reasoning is not effectively applied to other areas of radio and television, as I have always considered it a wasteful use of television air time to broadcast, for example, a concert that could be equally well enjoyed on radio – and where the sound reproduction quality would be superior.)

Teachers and pupils are supplied with a quantity of printed back-up material, for class preparation or follow-up after the programme, and in addition programmes can be taped off the air and played again or directly hired from the BBC.

Mention has already been made of the Schools Broadcasting Council for the United Kingdom which liaises with Independent Television on schools broadcasts and draws up the various curricula.

Schools broadcasts are planned in series and each is aimed at a specific target audience, at primary or secondary school level. There are currently some 125 series being broadcast, on radio and television, of which 95 are put out nationally, while the rest are distributed round the regions and cater for local needs and interests. Of this output, 33 are television programmes, 13 of them aimed at primary school children and 20 at secondary level.

As it is popularly believed that children are maturing earlier, the BBC has recently started a series of pre-school programmes, aimed at 4 to 5 year olds, either for viewing at home or in play groups or nursery schools. The programmes aim to assist (in the words of the Corporation) 'the development of language skills', though a lot of emphasis in these, as in most other programmes for children at this level, is on music and movement, mime, nursery rhymes, etc.

Children aged from nine to thirteen receive a variety of programmes, linked to school subjects as varied as life in the middle ages to assistance with French or other languages. As they get older, the subject areas broaden to include programmes of the *Job Worth Doing?* type with the emphasis on the community, work, social issues, economics, politics, etc. which older readers may recognize is a significant change from when they were at school.

The BBC and further education

Further education programmes could be described as the evening class of the air (though programmes are not broadcast in the evenings, as that would cut into valuable prime time) and their contents reflect the variety of studies, hobbies and interests that can be pursued on payment of a small fee at almost any local evening institute in the country. As well as providing programmes directly geared to further education courses – ONC, HNC and so on – they attempt to cater equally for the housewife who wants to take up crochet or gardening, fencing or musical appreciation, or what have you. As a result, the choice is overwhelming and if I have a criticism to make it is that because there is so much it is often difficult to find out what is actually broadcast and when, and because of the sheer volume of output programmes are often broadcast at incredibly inconvenient hours. For example, the Open University, which we shall examine in the following paragraphs, starts up at 7.30 on a Sunday morning and *Radio Times* does not even bother to itemize the various programmes that last until lunchtime on BBC 2!

Examples of the various further education courses on television include: *Engineering Craft Studies* for students taking the new craft syllabus and *Profit by Control* (business studies). *Man at Work* discusses the work situation, while *Workers at Risk* looks into matters of industrial safety. Some programmes are aimed at more specific groups, such as teachers (*ROSLA and After* and *Behaviour and Belief*, the second programme concerning 'moral education'), doctors (*Medicine Today*), or student nurses.

'General interest' programmes in this category are varied, including science for the non-specialist in a 'looking at nature' type of series, contemporary affairs, history, the arts, languages and family interests – community problems, health, parents and children, and so on.

Taking, as one must, a professional interest in television output, I must confess to having seen few if any of these programmes and series, for the very reasons stated above – too many of them are broadcast, and too little publicity is given about them. Surely many of them are worth repeating to a wider audience?

The Open University

The BBC broadcasts a series of lectures and other types of programmes in conjunction with the Open University, an independent degree-awarding body which started in January 1971, to provide part-time degree and other courses for adults unable to attend any other type of university. Education is by correspondence, group gatherings, summer schools, etc., as well as radio and television. The University is financed by fees and a direct grant from the Department of Education and Science and some 40,000 students follow the courses, of which there are around sixty. About twenty-five hours a week are broadcast on television (BBC 2) during 34 weeks of the year, or some 250 programmes annually on television (and nearly 200 on radio).

Children's programmes on BBC

These range from tiny tots to teenage and pre-teenage programmes and include the following programmes. *Jackanory*, probably the best known to adult viewers, is broadcast daily from Monday to Friday, and is basically a story-telling programme for children. Other series are *Magic Roundabout*, *Hector's House*, *The Wombles*, *Adventures of Parsley* and several others, which are variations on the puppet, animation or story telling themes.

Older children are weaned on *Blue Peter*, with its middle-class views of the 'world' as projected by the three regular elderly teenage presenters. John Noakes has achieved some notoriety for his various exploits, which have included sky-diving. One of the other participants, Valerie Singleton, has a

131

couple of additional spots, one is her series of 'special assignments' (visits to awe-inspiring places like Paris, London, Rome, etc., which the majority of kids had probably seen on school trips or package tours with their parents); the other is *Val Meets the VIPs* and into this category personalities as varied as Margaret Thatcher and footballer Kevin Keegan have been slotted, to be grilled by an uninhibited young audience. One child asked Keegan how much he earned, a question the young footballer skirted with all the aplomb of an experienced politician. And Mrs Thatcher must have come to regret her candid comments when she assured her young audience that she felt she had far too little political experience to become the first woman Prime Minister!

Serious controversial subjects are covered in *Search* (which I have never seen) and there are a number of quiz programmes (*Screen Test*, *It's Your World*) in which the junior contestants conduct themselves with all the seriousness of future Robin Days.

ITV and children

Because the BBC were first in the market it was inevitable that the independent companies would have to pinch some of their best ideas, and this they did in no uncertain manner with *Magpie* (Thames) whose format is identical to that of *Blue Peter*. ITV gives over a major part of its Saturday morning output to younger viewers, with *Saturday Scene*, a blanket title that covers American imported series, such as the *Partridge Family* (starring weeny bopper idol David Cassidy) or *Tarzan*, to pop interviews and records, the whole thing hosted by an embarrassingly 'young' presenter.

Sunday mornings, with the abandonment of London Weekend's *Weekend World* during the summer 'closed season' when news is assumed not to happen, are given over to the kids once again, with *Catweazle* (repeated), *Thunderbirds* and *The Jackson Five* (also repeated). Kids have the screen to themselves by tea-time, after the sports and film have made certain that their parents will drop off to sleep, with *Junior Showtime* produced by Jess Yates (the man who gave us *Stars on Sunday* as well) in which talentless youngsters are encouraged to sing or dance in a way that must be an embarrassment even to their doting parents.

The Sunday evening children's serial at the time of writing is *Boy Dominic*, but previous presentations have included *Black Beauty*, *Follyfoot* (note the obsession with horses), *The Pretenders* (vaguely 'historical') and *The Intruder*, adapted from the novel by John Rowe Townsend.

Weekday children's television covers films in *Clapperboard*, adventure serials (currently *Skiboy*), amateur science (*How*, a dreadful programme from Southern, presented by a group of TV aunts and uncles), imported series (*F Troop*, *The Wild Wild West* and *Pardon my Genie*), none of which is particularly uplifting or worthwhile. Only a recent series on preservation of wildlife is worthy of mention as a serious attempt at interesting children in something constructive, as opposed to entertaining them with comedy series (usually imported) or adventure programmes set in unrealistic surroundings.

Some earlier children's programmes from ITV companies are however worthy of mention, and these should include ATV's *The Jensen Code* (which featured the young boy from *Kes*) and *The Flaxton Boys* from Yorkshire Television. But these programmes have to be set against banalities such as *Little Big Time* (kid's variety), a stereotyped space adventure serial (*The Tomorrow People*) or *Get This!* a miscellany programme hosted by Harry Fowler and Kenny Lynch, surely two of the most unfunny people on television.

Education on ITV

As if conscious of their contractual obligations, the independent companies do rather better in the area of education, and about twenty hours a week of broadcasting comes into the category of children's and educational television. According to the IBA handbook, some 600 programmes in over forty series are broadcast annually, covering every age range from four to eighteen, but many of these are localized only, with each company producing programmes for transmission within its own area and not necessarily for the whole network.

At the IBA headquarters in Knightsbridge, the Education Secretariat supplies detailed information about children's and schools programmes, and also handles the 200 or so publications that are produced annually for schools, with a total print order of some $1\frac{1}{2}$ million copies.

Since the autumn of 1972, ITV educational coverage has increased with the introduction of a number of pre-school programmes for young children, making use of the midday slot (before the early news bulletin) to present either *Rainbow* (Thames), *Hickory House* (Granada), *Indigo Pipkin* (ATV) or *Mr Trimble* (Yorkshire); each programme presenting a medley of songs, games and stories, with *Rainbow* in particular making imaginative use of colour television techniques.

On Saturday mornings, London Weekend Television introduced the American programme *Sesame Street*, which – by US standards anyway – presented an interesting breakaway from action serials. Instead it offered a creative stimulus to children to do something with materials readily available from around the house – old detergent bottles and packets, newspapers, paints, crayons, and so on. All this is a useful reaction, too, against manufactured playthings.

In Thames's *Rainbow*, the programmes are linked by a presenter and a puppet bear, called Bungle. Each programme, like *Sesame Street*, is built around a theme – such as farm animals, transport or, simply, shapes. The themes are explained by other puppet figures playing well-defined roles – such as Curly and Straight, who are no more than animated lines, and Zippy and Mr Know-All.

Primary, middle and secondary school series

Moving up the educational and age ladder, the independent companies present a truly bewildering range of programmes for youngsters in these age groups. They range from *My World* (Yorkshire) about the world outside home and school (e.g. visit to a fire station); *Seeing and Doing* (visits to a farm); *The Magic of Music*; *Finding out*; *Figure it Out* (mathematics with Tony Bastable); *History Around You*; and *Stop Look Listen* (for slow learners).

Similar titles and themes are covered in the middle school series – *The World Around Us* (science oriented), *Let's Go Out*

134

(the environment), *How we Used to Live* (social history), *Play Fair* (community education), *Neighbours* (geography), *Living and Growing* (health education), *Cornerstones* (religion), *The Living Body* (biology), and *Matter for Decision* (youngsters in society). At secondary school level there are *Starting Out* (discussion), *Believe It or Not* (religion), *The Facts Are These* (social health), *The Time of Your Life* (social problems) and several others.

Adult education programmes are even more varied, but an attempt to classify them would show that most areas are indeed covered by, for example, the arts programmes, covering amateur dramatics, restoring antiques, painting and sculpture; English language and literature, public speaking; farming and gardening; health; history; leisure activities – angling, retirement, horse riding, bridge, judo, guitar, skiing, boating, psychology, and programmes for parents.

If all these programmes were available nationally, they would indeed provide a rich and rewarding experience for viewers, but so many are broadcast on a purely regional basis. *Fit to Last*, for example, was made by Scottish Television, and was an excellent series on health, diet, exercise, etc., that deserved a wider showing.

Children as viewers

Whatever the merits or otherwise of the programmes served up for consumption by children and young people, it must be remembered that their viewing of television is not necessarily restricted to the programmes and types of programmes specifically designed for them. It has been said that all television is 'educative' and this is for better or for worse. In the following chapter we shall examine the impact made, for example, of television commercials and the complaints by parents that they encourage children to be acquisitive, to imitate bad behaviour and to pester their parents to buy products that are financially out of the latter's reach.

As far as general programming is concerned, the broadcasting authorities have a special responsibility because television comes into the home, and restraints on viewing are not necessarily applied, either by the child or his parents. Unlike the cinema, which has to categorize its programmes according to established norms, television is free and requires the payment of no admission charge.

Obviously not all programmes can be designed so as not to offend younger viewers, and to this end the broadcasting authorities have adopted the 'nine o'clock' rule, by which most serious or controversial programmes are broadcast after this time (but note the mother's comments about earlier evening trailers in the following chapter, p. 162). It could be argued that the setting of the time of nine o'clock is a little early these days, particularly at weekends when children undoubtedly stay up later. This censorship by timing is occasionally applied by the IBA with curious results. In February 1975, for example, a programme on sex education of teenagers in north London schools was put back to 9.30 pm, thus undoubtedly attracting an audience of prurient adults in place of the younger people who were the central theme of the programme. It turned out to be quite harmless and no tits or bums were exposed.

Experiments have been tried, initially in the midlands area by ATV, of using a symbol denoting that a particular programme is considered unsuitable for young viewers, and this follows the practice in France and other continental countries where a white blob appears in a corner of the screen to indicate to parents that the programme being screened is not considered suitable for family viewing.

However, whatever restraints are operated, no early warning system will work unless accompanied by a sense of responsibility among parents. Sadly, the overall evidence is that everyone, adults and children alike, simply watch too much television, of whatever standard, uplifting or degrading.

The educational output overall

An examination of the overall educational output of the two services shows that there is undoubtedly a large body of people inside the BBC and the independent companies which is seriously concerned to put out entertaining and enlivening programmes aimed at younger viewers (and others). The people who comprise this group are advised and assisted by a whole mass of experts serving in an advisory capacity.

What is distressing is that here, as we found in an examination of the drama output of ITV, there is considerable duplication of effort, with the result that many excellent programmes are got together at great expense, but receive an extremely narrow showing. Regionalism is fine when discussing regional issues, but I see little point in the Scottish Television series on health being restricted to Scottish viewers alone – and then, as happened, London Weekend recording and broadcasting their own series. This is quite unnecessary and a waste of manpower and much needed funds.

I would also criticize the lack of publicity given to these programmes, particularly those not directly aimed at the school audience, where the machinery for supplying teachers with advance information and supporting publications seems to work reasonably well. All the adult education programmes described in the preceding paragraphs are broadcast at such odd times that it is unlikely that the casual viewer will simply happen upon them by chance, particularly if, like most of us, he confines his viewing to the evening or later evening period.

We are simply not yet accustomed to the idea of television during breakfast, and if day-long television has to come (and I question that it has) and these early morning slots, for example, are used for educational and informative programming, then a major publicity effort will have to be mounted to attract viewers to watch these programmes. Possibly fewer pages in the television publications could be given over to the private lives of showbusiness personalities and more space devoted to publicity for some of television's more serious output.

On the question of duplication, as air time is valuable – so valuable the broadcasters argue that each side is lobbying for the un-allocated fourth channel – television cannot be compared to, say, publishing, where if by some mischance twenty cookery books are simultaneously published, then the reader has a choice and only the publishers suffer if the demand for cookery textbooks is spread too thinly across so many publications. In television, we are dealing with a public service monopoly where, even if, in the case of ITV, the advertisers pay the piper, they certainly do not, or should not, call the tune.

The duties of television

If governments are seriously intent on advancing the cause of education and culture – by raising the school leaving age, allowing free access to museums, extending the library service, opening more colleges and universities – then a similar duty must surely rest with the broadcasting authorities, and we should always be seeing more and not less serious broadcasting. And as people's minds are expanded through wider education, their demand for a higher standard of television programmes must also increase.

Conversely, where even in the 1970s, as many as 75 per cent of the population have left school at the age of fifteen or earlier, there is clearly a duty to educate this vast mass of the population, in the broadest sense. As the report of the Social Morality Council points out 'there are no grounds for assuming that large numbers of people are born incapable of appreciating anything but undemanding entertainment'.

If in defence of their output, broadcasters argue that what they are offering is 'acceptable' to their audience (and point to the ratings by way of proof); they should realize that in pandering to the lowest common denominator they are appealing to human nature's innate weaknesses in giving the television audience what it wants. This is not something to be proud of.

Even if audiences cannot be made to watch serious programmes, this does not mean they should be switched to a minority channel (BBC 2 or the proposed fourth channel) or outside peak time. Audiences will accept and enjoy serious programmes, even when they view them by chance (perhaps for lack of an alternative) and it would be a dangerous situation if television came to be streamed in a way that radio output is now segmented by the BBC into Radios 1, 2, 3 and 4, so that listeners to Radio 1 (pop) are not encouraged to try anything more demanding on Radios 3 and 4.

'Streaming' in this way can lead to pressures on producers if they are making programmes for minority channels. Arguments can be used against them that 'their channel' is not paying its way and therefore budgets must be cut, and serious educational broadcasters then start to adopt second-class positions in the television hierarchy. The next step is a cutback in serious programme output in the pursuit of higher audience figures and the ratings.

Too much educational television?

In terms of licence fees, the schools taking educational programmes contribute around £250,000 towards the cost of the service, where the BBC alone spends some £6 millions annually. So the corporation (and the independent companies) are subsidizing schools broadcasting to a considerable extent. Clearly, then, there is a case for government subsidy, possibly through the Schools Broadcasting Council, the body that suggests and prepares curricula for broadcast programmes.

It is obvious that children's capacity to absorb information from television is enormous – witness any group of youngsters repeating or embellishing the various well-known television commercial jingles. But this is often at the expense of the basic skills, such as reading in particular, and the rate of illiteracy is truly alarming in an age when so much 'information' comes to us in pre-packaged form that is easy to absorb without effort.

There is also a tendency for local authorities to get carried away on the spending of vast sums of money providing the electronic hardware necessary for broadcast reception and recording in schools, and the ancillary materials – film loops, wall charts, cassettes – often to the detriment of books. It is interesting to note in this context that, as television continues to take steps forward in terms of satellite coverage, cablevision or viewer access, one of the systems being developed involves projecting a 'page' electronically on to the television screen, to appreciate which a basic reading skill will be essential! Television, then, should not be projected to children as the only source of information, to the neglect of books, newspapers and magazines.

A lot of what has been said about the scarcity of broadcasting time should be applied to the Open University project, which eats up precious hours on radio and BBC 2 for a maximum audience of some fifty thousand. Clearly this can only be justified if the idea of 'open' education is going to be extended to those with inadequate schooling and the whole range of programmes offered greatly extended to include vocational and

139

other courses appealing to a much broader mass of people. Criticisms of the Open University have already been voiced: that it caters for a minority that is well qualified already (teachers, professional people, though the occasional house-wife is projected as a sample of typical students), and is prob-ably able to get its education elsewhere, using the existing facilities of day release, evening colleges or conventional universities.

9. Commercials and Television Ratings

We have already noted that unless television is controlled and supported by government, as in the case of the two BBC channels in Britain, financial support has to come from the sale of air time to advertisers. As the seller of goods is keen to place his wares before the largest possible audience and at the most competitive price, he is not unnaturally concerned with the success or not of programmes reaching a wide audience. Because the advertiser is concerned with *ratings*, inevitably the television producer is, even, as in the case of the BBC, where the programme company is not selling advertising time. Ratings have in fact become something of an obsession.

The ratings battle

In an excellent examination of television advertising published in the American magazine *Newsweek*, the author quotes an executive from the New York advertising agency of Ogilvey and Mather on the terms used in planning television advertising strategy. 'Everything to do with advertising is cast in the language of war,' comments the agency man, 'The plan to sell a client's product is a *campaign*, the *copy strategy* reeks of a military offensive: is it a *barrage* or *one-shot* or *saturation* campaign? The people whom we are trying to reach are called the *target audience*. Doesn't it tell you something about the business?'

The volume of television advertising in America alone is some $4\frac{1}{2}$ billion dollars annually, most of it being handled by large, established agencies such as Mather, quoted above, J. Walter Thompson, McCann-Erickson or BBDO, most of them with offices in London and other world capitals and handling large, wealthy clients. Getting a pilot movie accepted by the agency's client can be a costly business – figures of anything from $4,000 to $250,000 are quoted – and a sixty-second commercial networked during prime time will cost the advertiser some $80,000 for one screening. So it is not surprising that agency men and programme makers are counting heads.

What is curious to observe is that this obsession has invaded the BBC in Britain, and they have an elaborate system of monitoring viewing habits programme by programme, and it is their system that we shall now examine and compare with that operated by the ITV companies.

BBC audience research

The objects of audience research are many and varied and include the following: the supply of background information about the population – number of television sets available and in use; the availability of people to view; the programme needs of the population; and their interests and spare time activities. One can then proceed to an examination of the *size* of the audience for television and its composition in terms of age, sex and 'class'; the flow of audiences from one programme to another; the amount of overlap between an audience for one programme and that for another; and the amount of programme loyalty that is generated; the general patterns of viewing and listening.

Research can be carried out on a pre-production basis – discovering the public's knowledge or ignorance of the subject about which a programme or series is to be made; the testing of pilot programmes (and commercials by the advertisers); analysis of viewers' and listeners' opinions as contained in the 300,000 or more letters received annually by the BBC and in the replies to the 20,000 questionnaires which BBC researchers send out. General audience studies embrace reviews of broadcasting services as a whole, reviews of *categories* of output (drama, comedy, music, etc.), and looking at minority interests. Particular audience surveys investigate reactions to specific programmes or series, the amount of 'gratification' experienced, and the short and long term effects of a quantity of viewers having been influenced by a particular programme or series.

From these various types of survey a vast amount of information is gathered and collated and made available to Corporation executives in periodical form, of which the following are the most significant.

The Barometer(s) of Listening and Viewing, two separate documents in fact, is issued daily, and in the latter case shows the percentages of the population aged five and over as the audience for all BBC 1, BBC 2 and ITV networked programmes, plus also some regional BBC programmes. There is also a Daily Chart of BBC 1 and ITV audiences, expressed visually, which compares the output, programme by programme, of BBC 1 and the five network members of ITV. Regional viewing summaries of programmes on all three channels are also prepared daily in each BBC region of the United Kingdom.

As if this were not enough, further tabulations are produced, breaking down viewership by age, sex and class. These tabulations are prepared twice a year in mid-winter and mid-summer, and show the amount of viewing and listening per head of the population per week to each television and radio service. It is in this way that trends are detected that might otherwise be overlooked in the weekly and daily surveys.

As well as being interested in numbers viewing programmes, the Corporation is interested in reactions and a weekly document is thus prepared showing graphically the reactions to some fifty programmes during the week. This information is then incorporated into Reaction Reports, which give a broadcast's estimated audience, details of its reaction 'profile', and the main results coming from the questionnaires returned with comments. About sixteen broadcasts a week are selected for this type of exhaustive research.

Weekly viewing and listening trends (all channels) are published in the BBC's Audience Research Bulletin. Most of the above information is available to BBC staff only, but a major survey of viewing habits, ominously titled, *The People's Activities*, is a 'book of charts and tables about the behaviour of the adult population from 6.00 am until midnight' (*BBC Publications*).

Estimating the size of the television audience is an exercise on its own and the two channels employ quite different methods to prepare their calculations. As has been shown, the BBC rely on daily interviews and questionnaires, while the independent companies favour the use of meters attached to a number of television sets, which record the amount of time the set is switched on and to which channel it is tuned. Both methods necessarily rely on *sampling* techniques (as obviously all of the population cannot be questioned all of the time) and we must first look at the basis of these techniques in the case of both BBC and the IBA.

Sampling techniques

The rationale of sampling is simple. If it is found that 10 per cent of a sample watched a particular programme it can be assumed that 10 per cent of the total population acted likewise. This is an over-simplification, obviously, and one of the first questions we must ask ourself of the sample chosen is, what in fact constitutes viewing of a programme?

The BBC argue that their method, using interviews conducted the following day, is the most reliable method of finding out who from among the sample actually watched a particular programme or programmes. Although reactions are not sought (at this stage), the interviewing technique does mean that certain information additional to the actual numbers can also be found, such as the composition of the audience – young or old, male or female, social class, and so on.

Further essential features of this type of operation are that the results obtained one day are comparable with the results obtained on another; the *whole* population can provide the cross-section to be interviewed, i.e. it includes those who may be found not to possess television or radio sets; and the informant is merely questioned about what he viewed the previous day (and not earlier).

It is not easy to establish who forms in fact part of the television audience for a particular programme. Are we to include the person called out of the room to answer the telephone or attend to the baby's cries? Or what about the family audience? The television set is invariably placed in the living room of the house, where a number of different occupations may be

144

pursued at the same time – reading, letter writing, talking and so on – while the television set is *on* (maybe even with the sound turned off). By using the interview system, the BBC argues that it can set clear guidelines for its interviewers about what does or does not constitute 'viewing', and if a subject being questioned falls outside these criteria, then he is regarded as not having viewed the programme(s) under discussion.

Other advantages claimed include greater accuracy of the results. The results are, for example, expressed as a proportion of the *total population*, as outlined above, and not as a percentage of households, and in their pamphlet on the subject the BBC show quite strikingly how completely differing sets of viewing figures can result from the divergence of techniques employed.

'Let it be assumed,' the BBC says, 'that 15 million homes have multi-channel receivers and the population of these homes is 45 millions, out of a total population of 50 millions. Broadcast A and Broadcast B are to be compared. It emerges that both broadcasts had TV ratings of 30, i.e. that they were seen in 30 per cent of these homes, that is, in $4\frac{1}{2}$ million homes.

'Now let it be further assumed that there were, as there well might have been, an average of 2·8 persons viewing each set switched on to Broadcast A (because it was very popular entertainment at peak hour) but only 1·4 persons gathered round the average set switched on to Broadcast B (because it came on rather late in the evening).

'This would mean that Broadcast A had 12,600,000 viewers and broadcast B only 6,300,000 (or as BBC audience research would say, their audience respectively included 23 per cent and 13 per cent of the total population). In terms of TV ratings these broadcasts would be said to be equal, whereas in terms of BBC audience estimates Broadcast A would have been said to have commanded twice the audience of Broadcast B. Neither statement would be "wrong". Their incompatibility would arise solely because the two methods were measuring different things.'

It will be seen that TV ratings and audience estimates cannot be expected to parallel each other.

The BBC sample comprises some 2,500 people interviewed daily, but even this large figure represents only one in every

25,000 of the population. As well as adhering to this number each day, the sample for the technique to be viable must be representative, that is, people of every kind need to be included on a systematic basis (children, teenagers, housewives, country dwellers, old age pensioners, etc.). One way of achieving this balance would appear to be using the technique of probability sampling, sometimes referred to as the 'nth' person. What is used, however, is the quota method, by which specifications are laid down in advance by reference to the known characteristics of the population, and the researcher therefore is asked to interview so many teenagers, so many old age pensioners and so on, to make up her quota. Social class, age, job, sex, etc. are all included as relevant characteristics.

The researcher is left a certain amount of discretion within these broad requirements and it has been shown that the techniques of quota sampling and probability sampling have over the years produced approximately the same results.

The actual work of interviewing is spread between some 200 interviewers, who usually work for a fortnight at a time, and then rejoin the pool of about 800 part-time interviewers retained by the BBC. They normally expect to conduct ten to fifteen interviews a day, occupying some two to three hours time.

Various checks are maintained upon the interviewers selected, including writing to some 5 per cent of the people interviewed, asking them to verify that they were in fact interviewed.

To assist in conducting the interviews, the researcher makes use of a recall sheet, which lists the previous day's broadcasts and the subject is further assisted by being asked to describe his actions through the day in chronological order. A subject is regarded as not having viewed a programme if he saw less than half of it, and researchers are asked to beware of informant's general knowledge about programmes, which they may not actually have viewed the previous evening.

The survey was initiated in 1939 (for radio), which means that a significant proportion of the population must have been interviewed by a representative from the BBC at some time in his or her life. However, I must admit that fairly extensive enquiries among my aquaintances have not produced a single person so interviewed!

146

The ITV sampling method

This operates in direct contrast to the method of the BBC. The only other continuous service of audience measurement is conducted by Audits of Great Britain Ltd (AGB) on behalf of the Joint Industry Committee for Television Advertising Research (JICTAR). The basis of the sampling is the use of meters attached to some 2,650 sets in various parts of the British Isles, which record the period of time during which the television set is switched on and to which channel it is tuned. In return for allowing the use of the meter (and completing various other formalities) the families chosen have their television sets maintained free of charge.

The results are translated into two daily curves for each ITV area, showing fluctuations from minute to minute in the proportion of sets tuned to BBC or ITV, and from this emerges the programme's rating.

When one considers that commercial television would be expected on the whole to be more conscious about ratings, in order to present accurate information to advertisers, the method is at best a remarkably crude one. Firstly, the number of households operating metered sets is extremely small, and also remains constant. Although users are not asked to alter their viewing habits simply because they have a meter, it would be surprising if they did not unwittingly 'co-operate' by, for example, leaving the television set switched on when in fact no one was in the room watching.

Also the results achieved are represented by numbers of households and not individuals, and allowing for an average of three members per household, the meter sample is seen to be smaller still – just over one third of the BBC interviewees, who are changing daily. Nor is there any reliable information supplied by meter showing the composition and size of the viewing audience, e.g. did the neighbours come round at that time and double the number of people gathered round the set?

By contrast with JICTAR, the BBC method seems on balance to be more accurate and more likely to be representative, and my only comment is to query why the state-owned system that relies on government grants for its revenue and is not dependent upon advertising, should operate this costly, if successful, sampling system.

Whatever method of audience sampling is employed, certain factors tend to influence the numbers of people viewing at any particular time, and these factors are not ignored either by programme makers or advertisers.

The timing of a programme will affect its 'popularity', in the sense that even a popular programme broadcast, for example, in mid-afternoon will not expect to attract the same number of viewers it would during prime time (7.00 pm to 10.00 pm). The audience can generally be increased by the technique of placement of programmes, the audience increasing if a programme is placed after a successful one or decreased if it is placed following one with a smaller audience. Audiences can be 'picked up' if the programme following is a popular one. Programmes are affected by the channel on which they are screened, and here BBC 2 remains a 'minority' channel to such an extent that large scale audiences do not accept programmes until they are repeated on BBC 1 (cf. *The Forsyte Saga*, *The Virginian* and several others). There is also the question of juxtaposition, so that programmes are affected by offerings on the rival channel. No documentary, however excellent, can hope to compete against a popular sports programme.

Some programmes are recognized as catering for minority audiences, but sometimes these minorities are quite large. There is inevitably a smaller audience for drama than there is for football or variety. And it can be argued that popularity is not just a question of numbers viewing but also of the degree of enjoyment had by the audience.

The BBC argues further, and probably correctly, that the 'ITV audience' tends to watch television for longer hours than those who are committed BBC viewers (and from my own experience certainly these two categories of viewers exist in Britain). Consequently any figures for comparative viewing will tend to favour ITV and not do justice to the BBC.

Measuring the ITV audience

The task of measuring the size of the ITV audience falls, as we have seen, to JICTAR, the Joint Industry Committee for Television Advertising Research. The organization in fact represents three other bodies: The Incorporated Society of British Advertisers, the Institute of Practitioners in Advertising (the agencies making the commercials) and the Independent Television Companies Association. The physical collection of the data required has been contracted since July 1968 to AGB.

In addition to the information recorded on the meter attached to a selected number of television sets (traced onto a special paper tape), JICTAR collates and analyses certain other information for its subscribers. This is gathered from a number of sources, including a master file of the characteristics of each household whose set is metered, records maintained in a special diary kept by the panel households, programme logs from ITV and BBC showing the dates and transmission times of programmes, a daily commercial log from each of the ITV companies showing the title of each commercial and the exact time it was broadcast, and finally a record of the current advertising rates obtaining.

Neither the JICTAR methods nor the BBC's daily sampling provide any information about *reactions* to programmes and here the two organizations employ further research techniques to measure the popularity or otherwise of their output. In this area, there is closer similarity between the methods adopted by the BBC and the IBA.

Since 1972, the IBA have made use of Opinion Research Centre Ltd, who compile information from a panel of 1,000 viewers selected according to statistical principles, based in the London area. In 1973, the scope of the enquiry was extended to include a postal survey from regions outside London, taken in rotation. Participating members keep a specially prepared diary in which they record their reactions to programmes, and from this an 'Appreciation Index' is compiled.

Mention has already been made of the BBC's 'Reaction Profiles' and these, and other information, are compiled from a panel of 2,000 viewers (and a further 4,000 radio listeners). Panel members are recruited either by advertisements or from among those interviewed in the course of the daily surveys and recommended by researchers. Whichever method is adopted, the composition of the panel is again according to statistical

149

principles, to ensure that, like that of ITV, it is broadly representative of the television viewing audience.

Panel members are supplied with weekly batches of questionnaires. These vary in content and form, the simplest of them requiring no more than a scale, linked to wordings such as 'interesting/boring' or 'funny/unfunny', etc., to more elaborate requests for comments and a general evaluation of the programme under review. The resultant 'reaction profiles' then show indices, expressed graphically, such as 'interesting/boring 80/20' and so on.

Both the BBC and the IBA also conduct various specialized *ad hoc* surveys, and also monitor public reaction to programmes as expressed in viewers' unsolicited correspondence, statements by public figures and articles written in the press.

Factors affecting reactions

Reactions to television programmes can be affected by a number of subjective factors, which need to be borne in mind when assessing the results of surveys. Included among them is the element of familiarity with the type of programme, the star or presenter; familiarity with the situation(s); the mood and intelligence level of the viewer; the amount of effort required to absorb a 'demanding' programme, and so on. Certain programmes appeal to certain well defined groups, e.g. jazz followers, so that a jazz programme might provide 100 per cent enjoyment for a limited section of the total audience (which might be still substantial) but provide minimal enjoyment for non-jazz fans.

The viewer's reaction to a programme may be affected also by his reaction to a certain part or element in it. For example, he may dislike the presenter whose performance is irritating, or conversely if a television play is 'enjoyed' the standard of acting also will be praised. Commentators refer to this phenomenon as the 'halo' effect.

Finally it should be remembered that the television audience cannot be treated as one man, and that reactions will be as many and as diverse as the composition of the audience. Frequently sharply divergent reactions will be recorded, but frequently, too, there is a broad middle ground where substantial numbers of the audience tended to think alike and the programme is said to have had broadly popular appeal.

It has been noted that nearly all the information gathered about television audiences is available to advertisers, and it follows that for strictly commercial reasons the advertisers will be influenced by what they discover about viewers and viewing habits. How then does this affect television programming?

Television and the advertisers

The Independent Broadcasting Authority, through its member companies, survives on the money paid to it for the opportunity to screen commercials, and every year some 20,000 new advertisements are dreamed up with the object of parting the viewer from his money. Because enormous sums are paid for buying a few seconds of prime time, it follows that advertisers are consciously or unconsciously shaping the pattern of commercial television.

We have already noted how this process has affected the evolution of television in America, where direct sponsorship of programmes is permitted, leading to the tailoring of content to suit the tastes of the advertiser. Because direct sponsorship is not allowed in Britain, the situation has not reached this stage, but one of the results of introducing commercial television has been an increasing emphasis on strict scheduling of programmes.

Because the advertiser wishes to reach the largest audience, the television companies have responded by providing programmes, particularly during the early evening period, that will attract the greatest number of viewers and build up programme loyalty throughout a series or serial. So between 7.00 pm and 10.00 pm programmes are generally undemanding and designed to appeal to the broad popular mass of viewers.

This tendency has not been confined to ITV. The BBC, since 1954, has fought back and allowed a similar pattern of programming to evolve, consigning serious topics to the BBC 2 minority channel or to such late hours that most people are in bed and there is no serious competition from ITV.

Advertising has contributed to the de-restriction of broadcasting hours, so that the IBA has more time slots to sell. The

BBC has been forced as a result to compete by producing more programmes with the same amount of available money (from licence income), at the same time as production costs are rising. Observers note that investigations among senior Corporation personnel would indicate that on the whole they would prefer to produce fewer programmes of higher quality, and simply be on the air for less time during the day.

As well as strict scheduling in blocks of thirty, sixty or ninety minutes, the commercial companies favour the series formula, usually in blocks of thirteen episodes, which have to quickly make their mark on the ratings otherwise they will be dropped or quietly shifted out of prime time. This means that accepted formulae, tried and tested over the years, are trotted out and there is little room for imaginative and creative innovation, which would allow a different type of programme a settling-in period before establishing itself with the public. In America this process is even more ruthless, with many of the autumn newcomers dropped or replaced by the following January, because they failed to make it on the networks.

Another more sinister influence is that of advertisers on the content of programmes, with their insistence that they should project what the Church of England Broadcasting Commission refers to as 'the television way of life'. Advertisers do not like to see programmes that present the harsh realities of life (*Cathy Come Home*, Northern Ireland news coverage), when this conflicts with their image of life as they project it, where a wonder drug will 'lift depression' or 'little things matter to a Birds Eye mum'.

Again this tendency has got out of hand in America, where advertising sponsors wish to delete all references to competing products and insist that programmes should be no more than innocuous pap that will neither inspire nor offend. This leads to stereotyped-formula programmes – the hospital series, the doctor series, the 'good cop' series, the cowboy series (witness the world-wide success of *Bonanza*), the domestic situation comedy (a quarter of a century of Lucille Ball under various titles, in both colour and black and white), the lawyers (*Perry Mason*, and others), the detectives (*Cannon, Banacek, Ironside*), mid-atlantic variety shows (imitated in Britain by exporter Lew Grade of ATV) and numerous adventure series (*The Persuaders*,

Hawaii Five O). Often only a 'star' name is used as the peg upon which to hang a series and in his *Universal Eye*, Anthony Green gives an amusing description of groups of network presidents lined up to meet major advertisers to sell them a projected series, linked to a Hollywood name, that could turn out to be cowboys or 1970s cops, according to the advertiser's desire.

'When NBC, for instance,' writes Smith, 'was kicking around ideas for a series in the fall of 1971 involving Jim Garner, they decided that Chevrolet might like to sponsor part of it. So a high-powered NBC team, consisting of Don Durgin, the president of the network, Mort Werner, the vice-president for programming, and Jack Otter, vice-president in charge of sales sallied forth to Detroit.

' "At that stage we had two versions of what the show might be," recalled Otter later. "Either Garner as a detective in a big city or as sheriff of a town out west in the early 1900's, but really we were just selling Garner." Chevrolet bought. They agreed to pay £1·8 million for three minutes of advertising a week on each of the first twenty-six episodes.'

Sponsorship is of course not allowed in Britain, and advertising is hedged around with all sorts of regulations drawn up by the IBA in its Code of Practice. We have already examined the rules (p. 60 above). How are they applied in practice?

The hard soft sell

I tape-recorded, as an experiment, a selection of television commercials throughout the period of two or three days, during the afternoon and evening periods. Some of these are reproduced here. They are not selected with any particular thoughts as to their quality or otherwise: let the words speak for themselves.

'Hygena QA is the easiest kitchen furniture you build yourself. Only Hygena QA locks together this way. Simple, quick, strong. So your finished units are really solid, home made (!) practical. And a kitchen like this costs just £169 plus VAT. And you can have it now. Go to your Hygena QA stockist. Bring home your new kitchen. In boxes – it could save you a packet.'

*

'These ladies have one of the biggest housework problems in the world – to clean and shine the QE-2 from stem to stern. So we asked them to try Sparkle. . . . We told them, as the dirt comes off, the shine goes on. They tried it. They liked it! Now if Sparkle can clean and shine the QE-2 in one night just think what it could do for you.'

*

'Buy a new electric cooker over £59 at your local electricity board now and get at least £5 when you trade in your old electric cooker. You can buy on easy no-deposit terms and delivery is free. So cash in now at your local electricity board. (Chorus) Your electric show. . . .'

*

'The Sterling Health Group makes many different pain relievers to combat special kinds of pain. From rheumatic pain to the natural pains of childbirth. And from Sterling Health there is a pain reliever specially made for headaches. Hedex. Containing the right kind of ingredient to make it powerful against headaches, yet gentle on your stomach. Hedex, specially made, specially shaped (!) for your headache. Hedex. Powerful against headaches yet gentle on your stomach. From Sterling Health. Family medicines you can trust.'

*

'From a remote island in the far Pacific comes the coconut oil . . . for Lux. Coconut oil as natural as the oils in your own skin. This coconut oil specially purified gives Lux its natural creaminess, that leaves your skin smooth and supple, soft to the touch. That's why the world's beautiful women choose Lux.'

*

All the above advertisements of products aimed at women – and broadcast during the afternoon of a weekday – were spoken by soothing, masculine voices, usually to the accompaniment of appropriate background music and scenery.

*

'When you are waiting for your baby to arrive home for tea

why not welcome him with his favourite thing . . . bread and butter and lovely fruity jam. Hartley's New Jam, a fruitiful way to any young heart . . . (Door bell sounds. Mother rushes to greet . . . large sailor-son. They sit down to tea).

' "Never had nuffing like this in 'ong Kong, mum." (son)
'Hartley's New Jam . . . a fruitiful way to any young heart.'

Note, here, the use of a build-up situation, where the viewer is supposed to be surprised by the arrival of the 'baby'. This takes place to the accompaniment of *There's No Place Like Home*. Voice over is rich and fruity, appropriately enough, I suppose. Note the use of the word *new*, which is quite meaningless, yet emphasized by the voice over.

*

The next two ads. relied on visuals to a greater extent, the first for Polaroid Cameras, showing two beautiful young couples out enjoying themselves in the countryside (appropriate music) and taking snapshots of each other. The second shows a youngish man in front of the shaving mirror, apparently trying to pick dirt out of his left ear, which he attempts to do with a variety of objects – corner of the towel, wet sponge and so on. His eyes alight on a packet of small sticks with cotton wrapped round the ends. His face lights up. Voice over: 'Johnson's Cotton Buds . . . for ears, and *things*.'

*

(Chorus) 'It's the right one, it's the bright one. . . . It's Martini. Any time, any place, any where. . . . There's a wonderful world you can share. . . . With the bright taste, of the right one. . . . It's Martini.' This advertisement is the one I probably deplore most, a straight appeal to the 'television way of life'. There are several versions, all of them featuring bright young things portrayed in exotic settings – water skiing, flying helicopters, driving fast cars (none of which occupations should be accompanied by alcoholic consumption to any great extent) – to the accompaniment of the Martini theme music, which also crops up in cinema commercials. Uuugh!

*

F

(Music, then Chorus) '. . . Ski, the full fitness food. For all the fam-i-ly. . . .

(Voice over) 'It's the dairy fresh Swiss recipe that makes Ski so nourishing for strong, healthy bodies. That's why every child should have Ski.'

(Chorus continues.)

*

'Here's one young woman who's discovered the ten-minute way to keep her dentures beautifully clean. Steradent (then plopping sound, followed by fizzing as dentures are dropped into tooth glass). Every morning, in the time it takes to wash, Steradent removes stains, dissolves film, kills germs. So ten minutes every day is all you need to keep your dentures the way you want them. Beautifully clean. Use Steradent. Ten minutes every day.'

Note the use of the world 'beautifully', implying that the wearing of false teeth (euphemistically referred to as 'dentures') is socially okay, and in fact may make you look even better. What about the lack of dental care that presumably led to the tooth decay that made the dentures necessary? Also, without the visual, the copy line could be applied to a lavatory cleaner or pan scourer with about equal relevance – cleans, shines, kills germs, like new, etc., etc.

*

'Even his *favourite* toys did not interest him. But now he's better.

"Is it a private party or can anyone join in?" (mother to young son).

"What they need . . . is Lucozade."

"Have they been ill and won't eat?"

"Yes."

"So they need energy to help them get better" (start of sparkling little tune, as voice off concludes).

'*He* knows Lucozade aids recovery.'

Here is an ad. that sets the scene that will tug at any mother's heart – sick child, abandoned toys, difficulty with eating – yet the advertisement really says nothing, beyond relying on the punch line at the end: 'He (i.e. the child) knows, etc., etc.' We are in fact told nothing about the product.

*

'Behold, the mighty Ajax bringing you his power'(blond-headed Adonis appears through artificial clouds). 'Ajax with ammonia, the liquid cleaner. To shift grease and really stubborn stains. And to get dirty floors sparkling clean. In Ajax pine, to disinfect as it cleans. And NOW new Ajax lemon, to keep your house and paintwork clean and fresh. Ajax has the power to clean like a white tornado. Ajax normal, pine and now new lemon . . . because Ajax has the power.'

*

'Ribena, the great natural health drink . . . for you, your children and your children's children.' Voice over a background of music, twittering birds and excited children's voices.

*

'Wake up to the SR tingle . . . and get a feeling as clean as cold, fresh air. . . . Get the look of sparkling whiteness . . . sparkling white, tingling fresh SR. . . . Nothing wakes you up like the SR tingle. . . .'

*

'There's a magic place where good children can have anything they want. It's called the Dessert Farm. At the Dessert Farm you say the magic word – chocolate turns into Choco-Mousse. A Dessert Farm Choco-mousse is true happiness, rich chocolate whipped with cream. . . . Say the magic word and all the Dessert Farm fruit yoghurts and cream desserts will appear.'

I object to this last ad. particularly because obesity is becoming an increasing problem among school children and yet here is a direct appeal to stuff themselves with still more calorie-loaded, sticky-sweet items. Curiously enough the next ad. appealed to slimmers!

*

'Helen has always been careful about her weight. In the last eight years she has put on one stone . . . just a small one . . . on

157

the third finger of her left hand. The weight watchers' breakfast, high protein Special K. For grown-up people who'd rather not grow any more.'

*

'The whole family use Right Guard. We all like it. It's the one they make for the family. It's the only anti-perspirant my husband will use. Gillette Right Guard is right for your family, right for you.'

Here is another ad. which tells us precisely nothing, other than that the product is 'right' for all of us. Notice also the use of the word 'they', the Englishman's universal generic term for everyone from the 'Town hall' to the manufacturers of soap powder.

*

'Mr Kipling's view about jam tarts is the deeper you make the pastry case the more jam it will hold. In fact he says there is one thing you can be sure of when you buy my jam tarts, they're just like we had when I was a boy – good and jammy . . . Mr Kipling does make exceedingly good cakes.'

Here is a superb example of a mass-produced item being sold as something individual and special, through the invention of the mysterious Mr Kipling (with fruity voice to match). The ad. for jam tarts was followed appropriately enough with another appeal to slimmers.

*

'(Chorus) Rye King is skip bread.' etc., etc.
(Voice over) 'Slender, healthy, slim and vital, likes to keep herself in shape, counts the calories in her diet, chooses Rye King. Rye King Slimlight. Slimmers' crisp bread. Light and lovely. Light in calories. Crisp as a whisper. Good and natural whole grain taste. Jane has a *liking* for Rye *King*. Slimlight – Brown Rye and Wheat.'

*

'Now, instead of tinned dog food you can feed your dog NEW Go-Dog. Go-Dog is a complete crunchy dinner with, ounce for ounce, more nutrition than any tinned dog food.

158

Go-Dog. Meaty tasting crunchy chunks that dogs really enjoy getting their teeth into. New crunchy Go-Dog. A dog's idea of a complete dinner.'

Again, I am afraid this ad. tells us nothing at all, except that the product contains more 'nutrition' than any other tinned dog food. We are not even told what it contains, other than 'meaty chunks'.

*

Keeping on the subject of meat, we then have 'the wealth of Wiltshire'.

(Voice over, with heavy West Country accent) 'Bowyers, for people like you and me . . . Bowyers for the taste of Wiltshire . . . Simple food, well cooked, country style. . . . Bowyers bring you the wealth of Wiltshire.'

*

Now another domestic cameo: father, son and daughter are decorating the landing, mother appears from the kitchen.

'Son: "Dad's right, we should have cut it first."
Mother: "They could do with their Bovril. Bovril. There's all that beefy goodness (!) concentrated into one spoonful . . . and that lovely beefy taste." (Family are now seen gathered at the bottom of the stairs in a charming group, sipping their Bovril.)
Son: "Soon be finished, mum!"
Mother: "Why don't you get the foreman to do a bit more work?" (indicating long suffering dad). (Final shot shows family group, now suitably revived, finishing the job, with dad pulling his weight.)
Voice over: There are times when only Bovril will do. Bovril gives you beefy goodness!'

This ad. is fairly typical of its kind, presenting a little scene from 'real life'. But rather like the pain-reliever ads. that show the tired housewife 'before' (lank hair, clothes in disarray, gauche, obviously not 'coping'), and 'after', we have the same device here: subtly, the son is shown making a poor job of fixing the ceiling paper. As they climb down for their drink, he is shown to have a stiff back. After a cup of Bovril, all is well

159

again, and the work is completed with alacrity, and there are smiles all round.

*

'Even the healthiest, most active bodies can suffer rheumatic pain. Fynnon Calcium Aspirin fights their pain. And because they're calcium, they're soluble and quickly bring relief that lasts for hours. Fynnon calcium aspirin.'

Here we have an example of the straight from the shoulder, 'medical' approach, with a voice over to match. Various 'healthy' bodies are shown in the visual, so the viewer is comforted by the implication that 'everyone' can suffer from rheumatic pain.

*

'Each medicated drop of new family Vosene now has a fresh new smell, a fresh Vosene, thicker now, to hold its medication ready till warm water gets it working, a freshness approved by husbands, approved by mothers. Regular washing with the medication in fresh new Vosene clears your family's dandruff . . . you just breathe clean hair. Fresh and medicated Vosene . . . the dandruff control approved by all the family.'

A good one, this. Note the use of the words 'new' and 'now'. Also implied 'approval' – by medical experts? No, by 'husbands, mothers, all the family'. Well, same thing, really!

*

Then we have what must surely be one of the viewers' favourites: the Fairy Liquid advertisement, which goes something like this.

'Revolting child: "I'm a witch with long scratchy fingers! And I can make you a witch, too!" (addressing elegant mum).
Mother: "Oh, now, I've got a good fairy to protect me."
Child: "Where is she?"
Mother: "Here, Fairy Liquid! She's all against nasty scratchy hands."
Child: "How?"
Mother: "By being gentle, with all these soft bubbles."
Child: "Soft bubbles aren't strong magic."

160

Mother: "Fairy Liquid's are. . . . Look they've got these eggy plates clean in a flash."

Child: "Lucky for you you've got her!"

Mother: "Lucky for you, too. Even witches like clean, soft hands, don't they?"

Child: "Girl witches do!"

Chorus: Mild – green – Fairy – Liqu-id. . . .'

*

We move on to another *new* catfood.

Soothing female voice: "All right, I know you want your dinner. . . . There we are. . . . Cupboard Love. . . . Something new, moist and tender. . . . Cupboard Love comes in foil pouches to keep it moist and fresh. . . . That's right . . . a new kind of cat food. . . . Tastes good, it's good for you . . ."

Soothing male voice: "New Cupboard Love . . . what the well cared-for cat has for dinner."

Female voice: "Would I give you something you didn't like?"

Here we have a number of ingredients: a *new* product, which does you *good*, is *good for you*, a *new kind* of cat food and finally appeal to the cat-loving instincts in us all. Who could resist? Interestingly, the whole of the female's speech is addressed to the cat!

Conclusions

And so they roll on, night after night. I am not suggesting that the IBA code of conduct is being broken (otherwise presumably the ads. would not have appeared) but at the time of preparing this chapter the media magazine *Campaign* revealed some startling results of a survey conducted by British Market Research Bureau about the effects of commercials on children, and quoted the comments of a group of housewives, tape recorded at the Centre for Television Research at the University of Leeds.

There were several conclusions: that advertisements deliberately encourage children to pester their parents to purchase products. Fifty-seven per cent felt this to be the case, although the IBA code states clearly that children should not be encouraged 'to make themselves a nuisance in the interests of any particular product or service'.

The mothers also criticized the lack of prices shown in television advertisements, and felt it was unfair for advertisers to encourage children to ask for things that were too expensive. This would seem to contravene the IBA rule that children should not be encouraged to ask for things which they could not 'reasonably be expected to afford themselves'.

The panel also felt that the code was again being flouted with regard to taking advantage of the natural credulity of children, particularly where other children were used in commercials, thus reinforcing the child viewer's conviction that what was being said was gospel. Strong criticisms were voiced about 'bad' children being shown in advertisements, such as the small boy who gets his clothes filthy and all mother does is smile and pop them into the washing machine. Nearly 60 per cent of those interviewed felt that children in commercials set a bad example.

While accepting that commercials were little more than a necessary evil, the mothers interviewed suggested that the bad elements could be counteracted with good examples. For example, advertisements for sweets could point out the danger to teeth (perhaps in the same way as the Government health warning on cigarette packets), though it should be pointed out that several toothpastes are advertised and are directly aimed at children.

Some argued that advertisements are calculated to make children feel 'inferior' if they do not buy the product advertised – in direct contravention of the IBA code on this point. Others felt that appeals to the child's emotions were commonplace; and finally the panel felt strongly about day time trailers that advertised evening programmes that were unsuitable for children, thus encouraging the youngsters to want to stay up and watch the later programme.

Altogether some 5,000 housewives were contacted for the purposes of the survey, and out of these 1,228, an effective sample of mothers of young children, were questioned. The results are certainly startling.

10. Some Aspects of Television

In this chapter we look at a number of current 'television issues'. These are wide-ranging, and range from the 1970s vogue for access television to the development of cable television, satellites and the fourth channel.

Cable television

Cable television, comprising systems where broadcast programmes are received at a central point and distributed to homes by wire or cable, began in Britain as early as 1925, as ventures and today they are largely in private hands – although they are licensed by the Minister of Posts. Today their function is to provide a form of commercial television, relaying programmes from the BBC and IBA over a cable network to the homes of subscribers and there are some 2,900 such systems in operation, with two million subscribers (some receiving radio only).

In addition to the licenses granted to the BBC and IBA, the Minister has granted licences to five of the relay companies to originate and distribute local television programmes, and they are: Greenwich Cablevision in Woolwich; Rediffusion in Bristol; British Relay in Sheffield; Radio Rentals/EMI in Swindon; and Wellingborough Traders TV Relay in Wellingborough, Northants.

The idea is to experiment with localized community programmes, which are financed out of the normal revenue received for relay services. The Woolwich experiment, which began transmissions in July 1972, has some 15,000 subscribers and programmes are transmitted in the early evening (repeated the following morning), and cover most local events – sport,

163

local council, the church, social services, road safety, the home.

One of the side-effects of the Annan Committee has been the curtailment or cancellation of many cable TV production experiments, owing to the large costs involved, and because no decision on cable TV is likely to be made before 1980.

In Britain, as we have noted, we are stuck for another decade at least with the choice of only three television channels, until such time as the 405-line transmission system is taken out of service (probably around 1985). As there are only twenty-four broadcasting hours in the day, it is not surprising that people concerned in television spend much time discussing ways of making greater use of the networks and of the electronic hardware.

There are 17·4 million television sets licensed and working in Britain, of which 5·9 million are for colour. As prices have come down, as a result of large-scale manufacture and the import of foreign made sets (particularly from Japan), the average cost of a standard black and white set is around £60. Many television receivers are of course rented, and here the service is backed up by chains of distribution and repair depots. It can be seen, therefore, that the investment by the public in black and white television is already considerable, without taking into account the total licence fees which provide the BBC with its revenue or the amount of money that changes hands between advertiser and contractor and keeps the Independent network in business.

It may be argued that perhaps we have got our priorities wrong, but domestic expenditure on television greatly exceeds that on, say, central heating – at present in only 34 per cent of households, despite our far from temperate climate – or telephones (around 19 million, but a major part of this figure is accounted for by business telephones).

In view of this, it is hard to see how cable television, which is more expensive by far to lay than a telephone line, will be capitalized. Nor where will the programmes to fill it come from. Let us look a little more closely at these two questions.

The demand for more television, if indeed there is one, can only be satisfied by investment in alternative sources of TV instruction and entertainment. The airwaves are already full up and we will have to rely on cable, cassettes or other means.

But the demand for more television should be viewed in the light of current social changes taking place, among them the increase of leisure hours, a possible four way day working week (early in 1974 we experienced an enforced three-day week, which was accompanied by a *curtailment* of television hours), and the increase in leisure activities generally.

As fewer people sit at home, expecting to be entertained, television viewing must surely be decreasing, as outdoor pursuits increase. There are an estimated two million weekly anglers, one million football players, squash and golf are enjoying an unnatural boom so that facilities have to be booked days or even weeks in advance, small boats are causing congestion on rivers and in marinas, and of course the spread of motoring means that more people are on the road, particularly at weekends. The boom in do-it-yourself is already a historical event, with more and more time, effort and money being spent on improving the home or on creative hobbies, and this is coupled, along with the car boom, with an increase in the number of second homes and weekend retreats – caravans, boats, chalets, camp sites.

On a more mundane level, more money is being spent on non-leisure items such as washing machines, dish washers and refrigerators, and – particularly by the young – on clothes. There is increased interest in food and good wine, and eating-in and eating-out. Holidays, too, are taken more adventurously, often abroad (nearly 10 million annually), and there is a trend towards longer holidays, and the taking of a second holiday during the winter months. Holiday makers now travel further afield, spend more, and require more sophisticated leisure equipment – ski outfits, underwater swimming gear, and so on.

All this would seem to indicate that Britons are living in a super-confident, prosperous society, but in fact the contrary is the case, and austerities of the early months of 1974, which brought a confrontation with the mining unions, a three-day week and a general election, led to a massive cutback in spending on such items as holidays abroad. It takes comparatively little to rock the economic boat.

There is, then, immense competition for the public's leisure spending money and it is arguable whether they will automatically fork out for sophisticated additions to their basic

165

television set. The TV industry, as we have seen, has enjoyed the benefit of a number of artificially created booms, with the advent of commercial television, followed by colour, but there must clearly be a limit to the amount of money that the public can afford or will afford to spend on further electronic goodies. Allied with all this, we must note the increase in the number of tape recorders and record players in use, particularly among younger people, and it is here of course that the spread of the hardware has been accompanied by the improvement in both quality and quantity of the product – music in all its dimensions.

This brings us to the second aspect of cable television. Given that the public were willing to invest capital in specialized equipment, enabling them to receive forty or more television channels in their homes, who is going to produce the material needed to fill the hours of screen time? As we have seen when examining television drama, experts argue that there is simply no more television writing talent available and that often directors and producers are forced to put out programmes that they feel do not quite come up to standard because of pressures of time and money, and the need to fill the existing television hours with anything. How then do they expect to produce material for a closed-circuit cable network?

Independent production companies

Perhaps the answer lies in access to television being made available to more independent producing companies, outside the mainstream of the BBC or the sixteen contractors in the ITV network. This is, or has been, the system in America, where little original programming was created by the networks, who bought in material from production companies. Unfortunately, in a system geared to advertising and profits, the results have been much the same as if the programmes had been produced centrally, with 'shows' being geared to advertising demands and audience ratings and, with the exception of the minority cultural channels, little imaginative planning has emerged.

It is arguable whether a similar situation would work in Britain. Certainly the talent would *appear* to be there. An examination of the film industry reveals that there are literally

166

hundreds of independent film makers who give up hours of their time and put their own money (one man even sold his home) into independent films, for which there is almost no viewing market. The industry is dominated, of course, by giant networks to a greater extent even than television, with remote executives deciding what the country will or will not see. As a result there has been a decline in the number of cinemas (to just over 1,500 currently), a fall in attendances (each member of the population goes on average only three times a year to the cinema) and a trend towards pornography and cheap thrills in an attempt to lure any kind of audience back into the seats.

On the bright side, though, the last four or five years have witnessed the opening of a number of small, specialized cinemas; development of film-making co-operatives, complete with their own distribution 'networks'; and an increase in the attention given to the National Film Theatre and the Institute of Contemporary Arts. It would seem, then, that in spite of the harm done to the film industry by the money moguls, the creative talent *is* there, and much of it could be applied to television production, given that it could find a method of entrée.

Possibly the most interesting parallel is with the music industry. There has always been musical talent around, but this was given a boost in the late 1950s by the arrival of the cheap manufactured guitar, an instrument priced within the range of almost any youngster who thought he had talent. At the same time, teenagers were born, with spending power that was not overlooked by the advertisers, and before long they entered the market offering records, tapes and the machinery to play them.

Record companies and publishers grew rich (one of them, Dick James, started in a two-room office, acquired some titles from an unknown group called the Beatles, and in 1969 sold his interest in Northern Songs to ATV for over £1 million). But as the music industry executives, 'the men in suits' (John Lennon), took over, creative people became more and more restless and dissatisfied with the commercial set-up and threatened to withdraw their services. Why, they asked, should we write/produce any more material at all?

The result of this new spirit is that by the 1970s the artistic

167

side of the business had completely taken over the managerial end, with artists flitting from one anxious record company to another, and dictating the terms of their contracts. A situation like this was bound to get out of hand, and stories circulated of huge sums of money changing hands for a contract, that resulted only in the group's subsequent disbandment and an abrupt end to the flow of creative material.

Clearly all is not entirely well in the music world, but the point is that musicians *have access* to the commercial exploitation of their talents in a way that television and film makers do not. The musicians' success means that more and more talent is poured into an ever increasing market, with the result that younger people especially are turning away from television and pursuing their own forms of entertainment. In spite of the fact that the record industry is tied to its own ratings in the form of the Top Twenty – and here the BBC panders to them with their ghastly *Top of the Pops* programme – none the less new and unknown artists somehow manage to break through and make themselves and their work known. They may not always be a success in strictly commercial terms, but their presence helps to enrich the musical scene.

Access television

Recent experiments in so-called access television have been tried by BBC 2 with their *Open Door* programmes, which were followed by a limited showing in the London area of *Speak for Yourself* (LWTV). There are, of course, other talk-in and phone-in programmes on both television and radio, and we shall examine these in a moment.

The trend towards getting in on the television act was probably given some impetus in 1968 with Anthony Wedgwood Benn's famous remark that 'broadcasting is too important to be left to the broadcasters', but what has resulted is not much of a shift from the position as it was before. Pressure groups, large or small, have always had access to television, though it is true that in the interests of 'balance' programmes of this kind have had a certain air of artificiality about them. Campbell Adamson (of the Confederation of British Industries) will be balanced by Vic Feather (Trades Union Congress), observed critic Philip Purser, almost as a matter of course.

My criticism of access television is that it is not really access in a greater sense than before. Television producers are wary of 'the general public': try ringing the press office at Shepherds Bush for programme information: unless a caller can satisfy the office that he is *someone* (journalist, researcher, aide to Mary Whitehouse or what have you) he will not get far. So access in other words is access for pressure groups, who would probably have been able to get air time in the general course of events on almost any of the other comment programmes – *Today*, *Nationwide*, *World in Action*, *Panorama* – if their public relations was good enough. All that is happening so far, is that the pressure groups are getting smaller, crazier, more specialized, but they are, none the less, 'groups' of people. I cannot consider access television as access in the truest sense of the word, until access is open to all.

Not unnaturally the trend towards access programmes has not passed without comment and examination by broadcasters and pundits themselves (worried in case they may quickly be out of a job?) in a series of non-access television programmes. Various views have been put forward, but the most interesting, I think, is the one which suggests that by opening the television studios to non-professionals, albeit with a certain amount of technical assistance thrown in, the non-professionals quickly become professionals, and who can then tell them apart from the existing broadcasters?

I am not offering this comment in any way as a plea for unprofessional presentation, which is what can result from much community-oriented, localized production. In much the same way as the poor standard of printing in the 'underground' press did little to enhance the quality of what was said, so badly presented programmes will simply turn viewers away, as they are used to a higher standard of presentation.

By gradually becoming 'professional' broadcasters, trade unionists, politicians and others who appear regularly on television, start eventually to lose their credibility, as they too are gradually viewed as part of the whole showbusiness panorama. As a result, the pronouncements of Len Murray start to carry much the same weight as those of Cliff Richard or Tommy

Steele (though the latter wisely has shied away from becoming a television pundit, realizing that notoriety as a performer does not necessarily qualify you as a moralist).

By the same process access performers will become absorbed into the television machine. On one of the discussion programmes mentioned above it was also noted how much more easily 'outsiders' took to the television studio, as a result of watching so much television. This is certainly true, but is it desirable that people should be copying a television culture whose values may be entirely spurious?

Write-ins and phone-ins

A limited form of access is the radio or television phone-in programme, where listeners and viewers are invited to call up the expert or presenter appearing in the programme. This formula has been cheerfully adopted (to excess) by the newer commercial radio companies in Britain, as a cheap time-filler, particularly during the early morning hours when the majority of sane people are asleep in their beds. The system has enjoyed a certain vogue in America, though it was found in one station at least that the same group of people continually telephoned and that effectively the programme was catering for an audience of less than 200 people!

I do not regard phone-ins as truly access television (or radio). They give an entirely false picture that the churchman or politician or trade unionist concerned is being put on the spot, for the experienced broadcaster can easily parry a disturbing question from a non-professional outsider. In any event, cut-off devices can be and are used (along with a delay mechanism to prevent 'obscenities' being broadcast over the air), and there is always a moderator on hand who sees to it that questioners do not get out of hand and fair play is observed all round.

Secondly, any one individual has a very small chance of being able to put a question to the expert or panel, because the telephone lines to the studios are blocked! One such American phone-in situation once jammed the entire Hollywood telephone exchange for an evening and Granada's controversial adoption programme (not billed as a phone-in) produced over a thousand calls, and led to appeals to write not ring.

Thirdly, phone-in programmes are necessarily confined to people with a telephone, and to those brazen enough to try to put over a point of view. There is no evidence to suggest that such people necessarily have something worthwhile to say or that their opinions represent a consensus among viewers.

What then is true access? In my opinion, a sounder form of access television would be an extension of the formal and informal procedures adopted by broadcasters for attracting people to initiate and take part in programmes. Viewers grow weary of the same old faces, so that programme formulae are predictable: social problem programmes will result in a call for Marjorie Proops and Clare Rayner; or, as a social worker complained to me, battered babies were in the news and because he had spoken once on the subject he had had ten or more appearances on television within a year, discussing a subject that had been a cause for concern to his knowledge for the past twenty years.

As we have seen, educational and religious programmes are influenced by quite wide-ranging committees and there are specialized committees that deal, for example, with appeals for charity on both radio and television. While not convinced that this system works perfectly, and considering that there is a tendency to call upon people who have already made their mark in 'public life', I feel the net could be thrown wider and more effort put into searching out and making use of expert opinion in the many and varied fields covered by serious television. A development in this direction would be a truer step towards access.

Instant personalities

This tendency for programme producers to go back again and again for the same people leads to the creation of instant personalities. Mention has already been made of this phenomenon in our examinations of news and current affairs and in connection with sports programmes. The tendency is a discouraging one, as genuine talent can be overlooked (see previous

171

section) and eventually the media start to feed upon each other. Let us look at a couple of examples.

First, Michael Parkinson: essentially a television presenter of a cinema programme and a writer and commentator on sports, Parkinson is the typical television creation. He has the sort of looks that apparently appeal to middle-aged ladies, and since a woman's magazine revealed that he had had a vasectomy operation, his sex life received almost as much publicity as John Peel's announcement that, yes, he too had had VD. Parkinson has hosted his own television show, which must be a sure way to meet people who will invite you back on to their shows, and so on. When I last saw him he was popping up on BBC 2's *What's My Line* (a curious middle-class revival, complete with evening dress) and plugging the fact that he was doing a book about footballer George Best.

My second example, incidentally, also had an operation, this time to transform James into Jan Morris. I doubt if many of us had heard of or even read anything by this person before the event, as revealed in the writer's autobiography, *Conundrum*, but the amount of publicity the book received in television and in the press was out of all proportion to the story related. Morris appeared on *The Book Programme* and then chose to be seen on *Talk-In To Day* (with Robin Day), subsequently claiming that in the latter programme she was made to appear like a freak, according to Katherine Whitehorn, who appeared at the same time. As a result of all the ballyhoo, the book, whatever its merits, managed to get into the bestseller lists.

The two examples are not chosen deliberately, but they are symptomatic of the present state of television (and other media, particularly the magazine world). What is discouraging is that people with genuine talent may escape the notice of broadcasters unless they do something 'different', and that public relations men are encouraged to stage manage events in such a way as to attract their attention.

Are we really informed?

This brings us to the question whether in fact people are any better informed now than they were before television was invented, and also leads us to examine the question of selection and rejection of news on often quite arbitrary grounds.

Writing in *Television and the People*, Brian Groombridge talks of the 'information overkill', and makes the valid point that amidst the mass of information poured out from television and radio sets the world over, the public still remains remarkably uninformed. Groombridge mentions various formal and informal surveys that have taken place, to try to establish some idea of the public's knowledge or ignorance in particular areas. Among these he cites a 1954 BBC survey that reported that, while the majority of the population understood the meaning of overtime, imports and retail prices, less than half understood devaluation and only a tiny minority 'terms of trade'. Twelve years later in 1966, two-fifths of a sample could not define inflation. In 1973 another survey showed that a sizeable minority of the public thought that Britain was already in the Common Market!

The reasons for this state of ignorance are several and varied. First, there is the sheer amount of information we are offered during the course of our daily lives, and not only through the medium of television and radio. Taking the BBC's *Nine O'Clock News* or ITV's *News at Ten* alone, each programme presents at least twenty pieces of new information every evening, of varying importance. This is the second problem. Because of the nature of news presentation, already examined, 'news' is reduced to a common level and by a process of selection and rejection, necessarily distorted.

As a result of so much 'information' coming from television the public are not encouraged to seek further and alternative sources of news. We have already noted that the decline in literacy is linked to the spread of television; for example, any survey among youngsters will show up a lack of awareness of national and local government issues that one would not find among, for example, French children of a similar age who happen to read more and are encouraged to question and discuss local issues.

Parallel with the spread of instant information is the use of jargon by commentators and its adoption by viewers. This happens in every sphere, from 'confrontations' and 'ecology' in news programmes to 'sweepers' and 'strikers' on the football field.

Writing in the *Daily Telegraph*, Sylvia Clayton cited some favourite examples from public figures, that included the phrases 'at this point in time' (i.e. now), or 'in this day and age' (i.e. today); 'something in the order of . . .' (i.e. about) or 'someone has gone on record as saying' (i.e. someone has said). And an MP remarked (on radio) that the problem of heavy lorries was 'something that has to be seen in the context of an overall national transport policy'.

As a result of Groombridge's 'television overkill', the public is at the same time over-informed and uninformed.

Actuality television

If viewers felt that the documentary drama had taken television as near to realism as was possible they were in for a shock when BBC announced their plans to film the daily life of an actual, real-life family living, as it happened, in Reading. The results were curious and again raised the classic problem of deciding which came first: the events or the televising of them.

In defence of the programme, the producers argued that the family chosen were subjected to an acclimatization period, during which they got used to the idea of having the camera and crews around the house, and eventually they were able to carry on as normally, arguing, shouting, swearing or whatever, as if it were not all being recorded for posterity.

The experiment had been tried initially in the United States, where it attracted high ratings but caused the family under scrutiny to break up and the son to embrace the cause of Gay Liberation. Presumably the broadcasters argued that this was a small price to pay for several hours of compelling TV viewing.

Another shock programme, transferred again from America, was Granada's adoption programme in which children requiring homes were presented on television. The programme was a worthy attempt to provide a public service and resulted in numerous telephone enquiries, but could be criticized on several grounds. It could be said that it did not offer enough information about the requirements for prospective parents – for example, that they should be aged over twenty-five, and that age should be related to the age of the child adopted, etc., and it did not stress that the real need is for foster parents (who take a child for a limited period only) and not for those willing to adopt.

The fourth channel

We have, as is well known, only three television channels in Britain at the moment and theoretically there is, or soon will be, capacity for a fourth. Even if there were a demand for more television (and the evidence suggests that there is not), broadcasters will have to examine the question of whether we can afford the cost of using additional airwaves for television.

Again it is Brian Groombridge who points out that measuring the 'power' required to broadcast in hertz or megahertz (i.e. one million hertz), to send out a high quality television picture with accompanying sounds costs some 8MHz (8 million megahertz), as opposed to the modest 200Hz required to operate a communications channel (for sending telegrams). So to invest in an additional television channel will mean sacrificing 2,000 two-way telephone links or 40,000 teleprinters.

The cost of cable television has already been referred to, and in terms of the fourth channel, enormous capital costs would be required, financed either from the government (through an increased licence fee?) or from advertisers if the fourth channel were to be allocated to commercial television. Setting up and maintaining the transmission networks for the existing three channels is already high, and since 1973 we have had commercial radio – although the Labour Government during its early days in office in 1974 hinted that perhaps not all the planned commercial stations will be opened.

All this must be set against the cost of servicing the new network, at a time when programme costs are mounting annually: an episode of *Callan* costing up to £40,000, and *The Persuaders* (heavens knows why) costs two or three times this sum. And all broadcasters will complain that their income is not enough to do all they can with the existing services, without the commitment of a fourth channel. Figures of £30 million start-up costs and a further £30 million annually (without allowing for inflation) have been mentioned as the costs likely

175

to be incurred by the fourth channel. In view of this, and taking into consideration the amount of filler material (old films, repeats, etc.) existing on the present channel, it is not surprising that the public as a whole are not enthusiastic about a fourth channel, and that most of the pressure comes from commercial and other lobbies.

The public's attitudes were surveyed in 1972 by the Centre for Mass Communications Research at the University of Leicester. Of the 589 people interviewed, 63 per cent opposed the idea of a fourth channel and even the remainder, who were in favour, wanted a different kind of television service from the existing ones. Of this latter group, 75 per cent wanted a minority channel, that would cater for specialized interests and hobbies, and broken down in specific groups; 32 per cent wanted local television; 23 per cent education and information; and just 12 per cent wanted more programmes of the kind already screened.

Before examining the various contenders for the fourth channel, it should be noted that it is considered doubtful that the Government would sponsor directly a new channel or increase the present licence fee to enable it to do so. Nor would it let the fourth channel go to commercial interests, though it seemed until 1975 that there is more than enough advertising money available to pay for it.

Let us now look at some of the claimants for this crock of gold, or barrel of lead.

The IBA and the fourth channel

The idea of ITV 2 has been around for a long time and, as already examined, the Government's rejection of the original scheme led to the de-restriction of television hours as a kind of consolation prize. Exponents of the scheme point to the competition between BBC 1 and ITV as unhealthy, with serious programmes being consigned to BBC 2, for which the IBA has at present no alternative.

Under the IBA scheme the fourth channel would be operated by the existing contractors, who would make programmes under the supervision, as now, of the Independent Broadcasting Authority. The channel would be financed by advertising revenue, and no levy would be payable to the government, all the funds going towards programming. Clearly there is a flaw here, considering the record of the commercial contractors to date, when many millions of pounds have gone out of broadcasting and been diverted by the contractors into enterprises as varied as motorway cafés and paperback publishing.

The IBA argue that the element of competition between itself and the BBC would thus be reduced, more scope would be allowed for experimental programming (education, community, access, and so on) and more work would be created for writers, directors, actors, technicians (though some producers argue that there is a shortage in these areas already). There appeared to be no shortage of advertising revenue available, as the de-restriction of advertising hours goes some way to prove.

Against the IBA proposals, it must be pointed out that, as with de-restriction, extra burdens are forced on the BBC who have to compete and produce more programmes with the same amount of money. It is likely that another channel would create more and not less competition leading, as it has done in the past, to spiralling costs, slavish attachment to the ratings, and the consignment of serious viewing, as at present, to off-peak hours.

A modified version of the IBA proposals was put forward by Sir Hugh Greene at the time of the 1972 Granada Lecture, when he proposed that the Authority itself would be responsible for making programmes and for selling advertising time, buying in programmes either from independent contractors or from among the existing franchisees. Revenue from advertising would come from the sale of advertising blocks which would be longer than the existing commercial breaks, but placed between programmes rather than in the middle of them as interruptions. This scheme is not unlike one of the suggestions originally made by the Pilkington Committee for the running of a proposed independent television authority.

A new television authority

Against this, various proposals have been put forward for the creation of a new television body to supervise and run the fourth channel. One of these, proposed by the Association of Broadcasting Staff, is for the creation of a national television foundation, which would consist of a body of trustees (appointed or elected) and financed by grants from the Government and other interested bodies (Trade Unions, industry, etc.).

Programming would be extremely flexible, with the foundation able to buy in material from independent programme makers, set up and finance projects, buy foreign made programmes, and undertake joint projects with publishers, universities, research institutes, and so on.

In his lecture, Sir Hugh Greene referred to this idea and suggested that a national television foundation could be incorporated into an ITV 2 network, allotted the same amount of air time during peak viewing periods as the other channel, and able to offer varieties of programmes for screening. Alternative proposals include linking such a foundation to the Open University set-up.

One of the problems of this kind of arrangement is the method of financing, and with this comes the problem of editorial control. A service of a similar kind has been tried in America with the National Education Television workshop, which was set up in 1968 with a £3 million grant from the Carnegie Corporation. Although it has produced a number of imaginative programmes (including *Sesame Street*), it is frequently bedevilled by financial problems. NET began in fact in the 1950s, more as an advisory service to local stations, and even then relied heavily on grants from bodies like the Ford Foundation. But the US Government has seemed unwilling to put money into NET, because of its freedom to criticize and attack, and growth has been retarded as a result, and more energies diverted into CATV (cable vision).

Reliance on funds from industry or other sources might lead to lobby pressures, which would restrict editorial freedom, and a great part of management expertise would have to be devoted to the collection of revenue and to assuring the continuance of the necessary funds. Without solid financial backing, standards of broadcasting might suffer (as they have on NET) and imaginative, long-term projects might not be undertaken simply because of lack of funds. If the foundation were to rely on advertising, then it would be forced into a position of competing with the other networks, and eventually end up putting out the same kind of programmes that it was originally created to avoid.

Given a successful means of financing, however, such as a direct Government grant paid for out of the licence fee, the creation of a third television authority is the healthiest of all the alternative suggestions for control of the fourth channel.

Other suggestions for running the fourth channel

Among these should be mentioned 'Television 76', a scheme put up by the institute of Practitioners in Advertising and the Society of British Advertisers. Not unnaturally, the proposition favours the interests of the advertisers, and proposes the setting up of a new broadcasting council, which would provide a public service channel, similar to BBC 2, and a fourth national channel for education and social programming. Against this would be set two 'general interest' television channels, both financed by advertising. The scheme has little to recommend it, as in essence it represents an extension of BBC 2 and the giving over of BBC 1 to commercial interests. Competition between the two general interest channels would then be heightened, as they both would accept advertising, and in turn this would inevitably lead to a lowering of programme standards.

Another proposal, by the Open University authorities, suggested consigning all educational broadcasting to the fourth channel, and the costs of running this would be borne by the Department of Education and Science. This would have the effect of freeing BBC 2 for more general programming, though this operates to some extent at the moment (BBC 2 only has the illusion of being a minority service).

Appointing a central, additional ITV contractor to run a second commercial channel has also been suggested. In this proposal the output would not compete with ITV 1 and no advertising would be carried: financing would be by levy on the existing contractors. This again would result in the creation of a minority channel, as inevitably popular programming that appealed to the greatest number of viewers would remain on ITV 1 where it would attract more advertising revenue. The

179

advantages of the single contractor are difficult to assess, if indeed there are any at all.

Proposals for use of the fourth channel as a localized network (using short-range VHF transmitters), while appreciating local needs, seem to be unaware of the extremely high costs of providing a television service. The danger would be in low standards of programming, compared with the output from the national networks, resulting in the creation of a minority, *local* channel.

Other alternatives include handing over the fourth channel to reports of Parliamentary proceedings (although the politicians are seemingly reluctant to allow this); and leaving the fourth channel more or less open, so that it could be used as and when requested by any competent programme-making body, and not necessarily be put to continuous use in competition with the other existing channels.

The BBC view is very much one of 'wait and see'. It is certainly opposed to allocation of the fourth channel to the IBA but does not seem keen to control a minority or educational channel. Without an increase in funds, clearly no extension of its services is desirable.

The fourth channel: conclusions

Clearly the decision as to who should operate the fourth channel and how it should be paid for is one that should not be rushed, nor need it be, in the light of the public's lack of interest in or demand for an extension of television services.

Taking a broader view, the establishment of a fourth television network (for whatever purpose, be it education or entertainment) means that money will be taken out of the national economy that could have been spent on some other project. In due course social planners will have to weigh up the relative demands of more television or extensions to the hospital services or more motorways.

Much the same broad considerations apply to all television developments, including cable vision already discussed. In this area alone, capital expenditure to provide coaxial cable (capable of carrying 60 programme channels) is variously estimated to be between £500 and £1,500 millions, at a time when the Post office is struggling to keep up with demands made on its telephone and teleprinter networks for commerce and industry.

Pay television

Pay television experiments have been tried in limited forms. Under this system, which is based on a cable relay network, subscribers can put money in a slot meter attached to the television set, and pay for a choice of programmes, such as feature films and sporting events. As far as the acquisition of programme material is concerned, pay TV is not unlike the methods adopted by cinema relay companies such as Viewsport, who acquire the rights to major sporting and other events which are transmitted live to cinemas or other venues, and audiences pay an admission charge to watch.

One of the dangers of this system is that a paying audience may enable the cable or pay TV contractor to buy first rights on important events which are shown by what is effectively a closed circuit system, while the larger television audience is denied the chance of seeing them.

Other developments

Other technical developments in the television field are mostly variants of the cable television system. In certain areas of the United States and Canada, these have been extended to incorporate 'answer back' facilities. These are not access type facilities, but by pressing a button attached to his set, the viewer can feed information into a central computer. This has been used by advertisers so that where, for example, a holiday brochure is offered, the viewer registers his request for a copy to be sent him, simply by calling up the computer from his set. Other forms of two-way communication are possible through this system, from calling on emergency services to shopping from the armchair.

Both the BBC and IBA are developing systems of data transmission, through their CEEFAX and ORACLE systems respectively. These make use of a 'printed page' which is projected electronically onto the television screen, and pages are selected by using a push-button method. Up to thirty-two pages could be selected and the device used with a normal television set.

Satellite transmission is already in use, for beaming instantaneous pictures from one side of the world to another. Satellites are also used for transmitting pictures over wide areas where provision of land lines or a series of transmission masts would be prohibitive. Because the areas served by satellite communication are less well defined than those of the transmitter, it should be possible for adjoining countries and those further afield to receive each other's programmes. This might not suit all governments, whether communist or fascist, but personally I look forward to the day when I can tune my television set to any station on the European continent, with programmes fed to a central relay point via a cross-Channel cable.

Appendix I
Two Major Reports

Occasional reference has been made in the text to the Report of the Broadcasting Commission of the General Synod of the Church of England (entitled *Broadcasting Society and the Church*) and to that of the Social Morality Council (*The Future of Broadcasting*). Both publications are recommended for further study, although I do not necessarily agree with all their conclusions.

The first report, *Broadcasting Society and the Church*, arose out of a motion passed at the General Assembly of the Church of England in 1970, when its Standing Committee was instructed to prepare evidence for submission to the Government in connection with the original Annan enquiry, proposed by Harold Wilson. Although the Labour Government gave way to the Conservatives within a few months of this resolution, the Church nonetheless decided to continue with its investigations and the Standing Committee appointed members of the Commission by early 1971.

The members did not include any professional broadcasters, and numbered Sir William Hart, chairman, a former clerk to the Greater London Council, and chairman of the Northampton Development Corporation; the Bishop of Liverpool, who was also chairman of the BBC's north regional religious advisory committee; the Archdeacon of Macclesfield, a former head of religious broadcasting at the BBC; Canon Harold Wilson, a former assistant head of the Church Board of Education; the Rev. David Martin, an author and broadcaster, a vicar in Kennington, London; Rev. Edgar Stride, an East End parson and a former columnist of the *Church of England Newspaper*; Mrs Kay Baxter, a writer and speaker on theatre and religion, and member of the Central Religious Advisory Committee; Mr Maurice Chandler, a public relations consultant who had spent some time at the Conservative Central Office; Mrs Jill Dann, a former mayoress and a member of the IBA's general advisory council; Mr Jeremy Murray-Brown, a former BBC current affairs producer (Panorama) and now freelance; Mr David Wills, a council member of the International Students' Trust, and on other committees; Rev. Michael Saward, a west London vicar, a former member of the Royal Television Society; and Mr Lionel Wadeson, assistant secretary of the General Synod.

During the period that the Committee sat, several important changes took place, including the de-restriction of television hours and the launching of local commercial radio. It was also announced that the BBC charter and the IBA licence were to be extended.

Twenty-six meetings were held by the Committee, of which eight were 'residential' and involved two or three days' continuous discussion. Written and oral evidence was taken from a wide range of organizations and individuals and some research was undertaken to assist the Commission by the Centre for Mass Communication Research at Leicester University. Visits were made to BBC and ITV studios, and to the centres for television training of the clergy. Opinions were also taken from congregations in nine dioceses, mainly through meetings and discussions.

The main conclusions of the Report were:

1. Broadcasting does not simply reflect the attitudes of society but helps to form them. It follows that producers cannot be neutral or disclaim responsibility for the attitudes they help to propagate.

2. It was not obvious to members of the Commission that more television is needed, or indeed that we needed as much as there currently is.

3. Even when purporting to describe events, the television screen may mislead, in so far as events are conditioned by the medium and have been subjected to a selection process.

4. The advertising element helps to create unrealistic desires and ambitions, which can breed discontent and deaden our sense of responsibility for the real needs of the world.

5. Commercial television's overriding concern with financial returns has deeply affected the BBC's attitudes and programming, and has led the public service Corporation to compete for mass audiences at the expense of other considerations.

6. Further investigations will have to be made in the study of broadcasting after 1981. There could be a case for pooling of broadcasting revenue through the agency of one public authority.

7. Other responsibilities of such an authority would include public accountability and research into the effects of television.

8. No decision as to the future of broadcasting after 1981 should be taken without public enquiry.

9. No decision should be made at this stage on the fourth channel.

10. Alternatives to the BBC and IBA, however, should be examined.

11. In view of the foregoing, the franchise for the fourth channel should not be given to the IBA companies, but might be allotted to the IBA itself in some new form.

12. Christian opinion should be alerted to make immediate use of opportunities to consider Government proposals.

13. The Commission was divided on whether or not a Broadcasting Council should be established, and felt that certain aspects that some members felt should be handled by such a Council could in fact be handled by existing bodies, e.g. complaints by the Press Council, and fuller use of the existing advisory bodies.

14. Programmes not considered suitable for family viewing should not be screened before 10.00 pm.

15. Careful assessment needed of the ATV experimental 'white dot' warning symbol.

16. The Commission welcomed the BBC study on taste and standards in broadcasting.

17 to 38. Concerned religion and broadcasting, including the use made of religious programmes, training of clergy for television, and so on, and are outside the scope of this general survey.

As mentioned, additional surveys were undertaken by the Centre for Mass Communications Research, and the following is a summary of their most important findings.

1. Of the 550 people interviewed, a majority wished to see some change in television programme content, but opinions frequently cancelled each other out, leaving researchers with the impression that, on the whole, viewers were broadly satisfied with what they got.

2. 45 per cent of the sample regarded the provision of news and information as the most important function of television, with 40 per cent opting for entertainment, and 15 per cent for education. Half the people interviewed regarded television as the most important source of news.

3. 70 per cent were happy with the licence system as applied to the BBC and 70 per cent had no objection to advertising on ITV.

4. Most felt that broadcasters were good judges of public taste and felt that they were able to make their views known, but fewer than 3 per cent had ever in fact done so.

5. As mentioned already, 63 per cent rejected the need for a fourth channel.

6. Detailed analyses of programmes brought some interesting responses, among them: that fictional programmes were limited in range (adventure, soap opera, situation comedy) and relied heavily on crime, violence and relations between the sexes; roles were relatively conventional, and the middle classes were featured in

185

preference to working-class people, violence occurred in most pro-grammes, with a high percentage (89 per cent) of American pro-grammes featuring violence.

7. Use of film for news broadcasting is important, as only 14 per cent of news programmes relied on newscaster alone. Heavy con-centration (63 per cent) on home news, of which 50 per cent were political and economic items.

The second report, *The Future of Broadcasting*, was compiled by the Social Morality Council, a body of which I must confess I had not heard, but which describes itself as bringing together 'humanists and religious believers of various faiths to search for common ground and undertake joint studies of contemporary social issues'.

The Report was commissioned in 1972 and the members gave evidence in their private capacities and not as members of the organizations they represented. Certain issues were deliberately ex-cluded, including those covered by the Church's report and a report on conditions of employment undertaken by the Association of Cinema and Theatre Technicians, and the members are listed by name only.

They were: Dame Margaret Miles, Dame Elizabeth Ackroyd, Father Agnellus Andrew, Catherine Avent, Dr J. G. Blumler, Mr Jeremy Bray, Rt. Hon. Lord Brown, Dame Anne Bryans, Sir Ronald Gould, Alan Hill, Rev. Douglas Hubery, Dipak Nandy, J. G. Owen, Stella Richman, Jean Rowntree, John Scupham, Jack Straw, Rev. O. Tomkins, Oliver Whitley, Rev. John Harriott, S.J., and Janet Mortimer. A number of 'observers' also took part, including Ian Alexander (from the Foreign and Commonwealth Office), L. J. Burrows (Department of Education and Science), Col. Robert Hornby, Dennis Lawrence (Ministry of Posts and Telecommunications) and Edward Oliver, of the Social Morality Council.

The Report is extremely thorough and comprehensive, examining first of all, the goals of broadcasting, and then the structures of broadcasting – including the issues of the fourth channel and the development of cable vision. A major section then deals with accountability and a further one looks at broadcasting and education.

The Report's main recommendations can be summarized as follows:

1. A national Centre for Broadcasting is needed, independent of both the government and broadcasting institutions.

2. Broadcasters should preserve their independence.

3. The aims of broadcasting should include broadcasting as an instrument 'for encouraging participatory democracy'.

4. Long-term research is needed into the social effects of broadcasting.

5. Further study and debate are required about the need for a fourth channel and how it should be allocated, if such a need be proved. (A minority favoured allocation to the IBA.)

6. At least one-third of peak viewing time should be allocated to educative and informative programming.

7. Cable systems require further study and should be confined to local, community and educational needs.

8. The IBA should offer greater incentives towards regional programming.

9. Further study is recommended of the ways in which advertising time is regulated by foreign services.

10. A proportion of the broadcasting levy should be earmarked for improvements to programming.

11. At least one-third of the General Advisory Councils should be appointed independently of the broadcasting institutions.

12. BBC should improve its internal and external consultative procedures.

13. BBC should be less defensive and more prepared to divulge results of its research.

14. Increase in the licence fee is necessary, and could be supplemented by special grants, e.g. for education programmes.

15. A majority favoured setting up a Complaints Review Board to consider charges of inaccuracy and misrepresentation.

16. Consideration should be given to a new agency to oversee educational broadcasting.

17. Schools should be adequately supplied with audio-visual equipment and teachers trained in its use.

18. Communications media should be studied as part of school curricula.

Appendix II
Television and the Critics

One of the fascinating things about compiling a book of this sort is that the author is obliged to research into what everyone else has said about the subject of television, and no source of comment, criticism and approval is more varied and colourful than the writings of the serious television critics.

Outside the popular daily newspapers, the television critics form an impressive body of opinion, and in this short appendix, I propose to show examples of what I consider some of their best work. Most of the comments are from writers on the *Guardian, Daily Telegraph, The Times, Sunday Times, Observer* and *Sunday Telegraph.*

1. Two views of a *Play for Today*

(The play, *Easy Go,* was about a group of East End youngsters trying to salvage an old copper boiler from the Thames, in the face of competition from a group of dockers).

The *Daily Telegraph* (Richard Last) condescendingly headlined its piece 'Easy pictorialisation of East End play', and went on:

'This time the protagonists were *an engaging bunch of East End teenagers,* totally without student self consciousness and self indulgence, and I found the film considerably more sympathetic than its predecessor.' (*Italics mine.*)

Peter Dunn in the *Sunday Times* was more down to earth.

'This story of a group of children in Deptford,' he wrote, 'trying to salvage a copper boiler from the Thames took full visual advantage of the river's dockland scenery. The children ran everywhere, Lilliputian figures dodging under the bulk of stranded barges, totally absorbed in their task. In victory they lost the boiler to a couple of big dockers who gave them a shove in the face before carting the prize off to the scrap yard – an early lesson in the unacceptable face of capitalism, no doubt.'

2. Two views of *Parkinson*

First, Richard Last again, in the *Telegraph,* under a heading ' "Parkinson" needs pensioning off':

'If there are any new ideas floating about in television this autumn, they must have been quietly suppressed or lost in transit. Here we go again with *Parkinson* (BBC 1). . . .

'*Parkinson,* the programme, not the individual, seems to me a right candidate for pensioning off. This I recall was the chat show that was *never* going to be a mere forum for actors, telling us about their last film and puffing their next.

'So on Saturday we kicked off with two American actors, one dark and inarticulate, and the other fair and inarticulate, talking about their work, past, present and in progress.

'The statement is almost an exaggeration: Parkinson had to work like a beaver through his stereotyped catechism ("which of the old stars do you most admire?") to get a coherent sentence out of either of them.

'Through inadvertence or indifference, he has got himself caught in the old trap once raised to a cult by Eamonn Andrews, of supposing that because actors are trained in delivering other people's words they must have plenty of their own.

'The farce was heightened by the arrival of Al Capp, a truculent, witty and highly articulate American conservative, looking for argument. You hear the producer's mind at work: "Three Americans talking about America, oh, great." It wasn't. It was pathetic. The entertaining Mr Capp needed matching – not for "balance" just for conversation – with someone of opposed ideas, but equal weight.

'But that would make *Parkinson*, which is a baby of the BBC's Light Entertainment department, a different kind of programme, and Parkinson redundant.'

In the *Daily Mail*, Virginia Ironside wrote:

'Compèring a chat show must be much the same as playing leader to a group therapy session.

'The idea is to lure your guests/patients down alleys they wouldn't dare go down alone, then jump on them in the dark and watch their reaction: lull them into confidences they wouldn't dream of telling normally, and then make them forget they are confiding in millions of viewers.

'Michael Parkinson, unlike the therapist or *Man Alive*, is prevented from succeeding in this task, like all chat show compères, by time.

'Instead, as in his return with *Parkinson* (BBC 1), he plays the part like a racing driver, anticipating every answer to his questions, already forging the next move seconds in advance, swerving to keep his guests on the track he has decided for them.

'In Elliot Gould and Donald Sutherland he had a right couple of dummies. In spite of their boring, impudent, American lolling and refusal to answer questions, Parkinson soldiered on, eyes steely behind a relaxed grin.

'In this show I thought Parkinson was the biggest star.

'He may introduce his guests preposterously (Al Capp was compared to Dickens, Dante, Mark Twain and a pile of others, and turned out to be an average American loud-mouth) but you feel he has got them all pretty much taped.'

3. Two views of Hefner

Yorkshire television presented a documentary of Hugh Hefner, founder of the Playboy organization. Producer was Tony Palmer.

Clive James wrote in the *Observer*:

'Mocking Hefner is easy to do and in my view should be made easier: as editor of *Playboy* and controller of its merchandising empire, he emanates an intensity of solemn foolishness which is no less toxic for calling itself liberating. I would have enjoyed the show more if Palmer had been in love with his subject less. There was a tendency to take the Hefnerite nexus of activities at its self-proclaimed value. Siegfried's funeral march crashed out heroically on the sound track where 'My Ding-a-Ling' would have been more appropriate, and the camera drooled like a Pavlov dog as it was led about in Hef's de luxe ambience.

' "I live the kind of life surrounded by beautiful things, female and material." Hefner's use of language was extraordinary. Approving new layouts for the "What kind of man reads *Playboy*?" series of ads he liked the one "where the man is showing off the artefact to his date". Further afield, in such outposts of Hefner's empire as the London Playboy Club, the film making got more sardonic. There was no gainsaying the fact that to make it as a Bunny a girl needs more than just looks. She needs idiocy, too. Otherwise there'd be no putting up with the callous fatuity of the selection process.

'An aspiring Playmate was given a ride in a limousine and told that she would feel honoured, because being given a ride in a *Playboy* limousine was really exciting. What did she think? "It's rilly exciting." Did she feel honoured? "I rilly do." We were shown the finer points of the Bunny Dip, which is the technique a waitress uses to bend down without springing out of her wired costume like an auto-inflated life raft.

' "Our notion," averred Hefner, "was that a total man ought to have a part of his life that could be described as a playboy attitood." Total Man, showing off the artefact to his date.'

In the *Sunday Times*, Peter Lennon wrote:

'At one point in *The World of Hugh Hefner* (Yorkshire) we see this raw-boned master of the *Playboy* empire squatting on a luxurious circular bed, a blonde by his ankle, surrounded by expensive junk. He lifts a telephone and his grave statement is: "I'd like a couple of ham sandwiches and some iced tea."

'This meaningless scene of consumer luxury carrying a hint of eroticism, in which the man is shadowy and the woman mute, from which we get no useful information of any kind, is characteristic of Tony Palmer's film. It is essentially a commercial: it has the commercial's deceptive gloss, the spinelessness, the capacity to conceal all reality.

'It neither tells us anything useful about Hefner's business world, nor does it reveal anything at all about that area in which he claims to be expert – his erotic world. The one area of interest might have been the marketing methods of this $200 million enterprise, but the film tells us nothing about this either.

'Hefner's claim to have liberated America's puritanism is, of

190

course, rubbish: he deals in a very infantile level of eroticism which has always been well within the tolerance of the average American. He shies away from the coarse physical honesty of a Henry Miller and no sense of joy emanates from his pasteurised prurience.

'While he indulges in what is apparently his idea of fun, playing Monopoly or table football with the boys, the women are hung around the room like Christmas decorations.

'It is frequently possible to be critical of a person by simply allowing him to make revealing statements about himself: with Hefner we were only allowed to hear grave banalities. When the film touched upon what might have been a real relationship, his attitude to his children, it instantly moved evasively from it, and the only statement that might have been revealingly developed was immediately contradicted: Hefner said that he had had a happy and emotionally fulfilled childhood – and in the same breath that his father had left him alone so much that he had retired into a world of his own and wrote stories for himself.

'Tracking over scenes of culinary luxury, along lanes of stereo equipment, drifting over mountains and skyscrapers alongside Hefner's black jet, Tony Palmer's camera was essentially servile when it could have been critical and ironic. (If, that is, Hefner had not had the last word in vetting and launching the film.) The final triumphant litany of the commercial achievements of the *Playboy* empire underlined the scandal that at this time of restrictions on television such an hour-long commercial, celebrating luxurious sterility, should have been allowed on the air.'

4. A comment on *Napoleon and Love*

'*Napoleon and Love* is so startlingly awful that it could well become a collector's piece, the kind of programme you watch week by week to see if each new episode has maintained or surpassed the fatuity of the last.

'Not even Thames, surely, can believe that these preposterous puppets have any connection with the historical Napoleon or his entourage, that scourge and admiration of all Europe.

'From first to last, with the possible exception of T. P. McKenna's performance as Barras, there isn't a shred of anything that could be called period atmosphere. The whole provenance is of a contemporary television soap opera decked out in hired costumes.

'The most remarkable thing about *Napoleon and Love*, surpassing the vulgarity of Philip Mackie's script, is the acting. When one considers the names in the cast, its badness is incredible.'

(*Telegraph*)

191

5. Friday nights on ITV

A comment by Nancy Banks-Smith (*Guardian*):

' "This is London Weekend with great entertainment for every-one." On Fridays, "Everyone" is of course that burden on the welfare state the Go-to-bed family. Kev, Gary, Cheryl and Gran.

'Kev really reckons *The Adventurer* being a right comic fan. Heroes like The Incredible Wreck who are by day mild mannered accountants and dialogue such as Ker Pow and Aarhgargr! This may be because Kev has some difficulty in reading, him being a late developer. *The Adventurer* suits him very well, being about Gene Bradley who is, by day, a mild mannered millionaire, and discovered last night he was being impersonated by a nameless thing in a mask. (Nameless because whoever it was did not get a credit in the cast list.)

'The last five minutes were filled, as they always are, with a free for all fist fight. The kind of dialogue Kev understands "you are all going to end up very, very dead". And the kind of sounds that are music to his rather cauliflowered ear. Ker-runch . . . Eek! and extraordinarily Ker-plosh! the sound of a fist meeting a face. I think this may have been misread by sound effects as it sounds precisely like a fish meeting a face.

'The highly horrible *Hawaii Five-O* is evidently intended for Kev's horrible brother Gary. He likes to spray the screen with slogans like Bovver for ever, from his little black paint aerosol. This makes viewing difficult for Mum who last night could not get a good view of the goat on *Sez Les* (Yorkshire) which made a contribution to (or criticism of) the show. I thought the goat over critical myself.

'I cannot imagine who watches *Within these Walls* (LWTV) unless it is Cheryl, who often says she'd like to be a screw. At least I think that is what she says. The horror film, *The Curse of the Crimson Altar*, is evidently meant for Gran-go-to-bed who never does go to bed and insists that she is really sitting up to see *The Bible Comes to Life* (Bill Medcalf looks at the function of the synagogue in Jewish life) at midnight.'

6. Some views of Margaret Thatcher

The February 1975 Tory Party leadership elections offered tele-vision some ready-made personalities among the contenders, among them Margaret Thatcher, who eventually came out on top. Tele-vision and the critics were not kind to her.

Writing in the *Observer*, Clive James:

'Visually she has few problems. The viewer, according to his prejudices, might or might not go for her pearls and twin-sets, and the hairstyles are sheer technology. But the camera loves the face and the face is learning to love the camera back. She is rapidly becoming an adept at helping a film crew to stage a fake candid. While her excited daughter unleashes a hooray bellow in the background, and her husband Mr Mystery vaults out of the window or barricades himself in the bathroom, the star turn is seen to be reading the newspapers with perfect casualness, right in focus.

'The hang-up has always been the voice. Not the timbre so much as, well, the *tone* – the condescending explanatory whine which treats the squirming interlocutor as an eight-year-old child with personality deficiencies. It has been fascinating recently to watch her striving to eliminate this. BBC 2 *News Extra* on Tuesday night rolled a clip from May 1973 demonstrating the Thatcher sneer at full pitch. (She was saying that she wouldn't *dream* of seeking the leadership.) She sounded like a cat sliding down a blackboard.'

Peter Lennon in the *Sunday Times*:

'. . . When a tractor raised a pile of garbage recklessly over her head she stopped it with a jolly hockey command "Steady on there" and continued to happily pace the mud with the gaffer.

'But then from the left of the frame came an unsummoned stooping creature who began to wipe her shoes. Dab, dab, wipe, wipe, he went while Mrs Thatcher gave a silvery, uncertain laugh and cried out: "This has never happened to me before" while she no doubt debated whether to hurriedly withdraw her tailored toecap or bury it in the ribs of this obsequious chiropodist.

'Later, back home with hubby, son and daughter, she spoke with quiet dignity of law and order, the punishment fitting the crime, and allowing people the wonderful privilege of surviving with the help of their loving families. "I don't help during elections" piped up her daughter, who was manifestly a chip off the old Dresden. Mother said evenly that daughter's contribution at election time was to keep the house going. Daughter then fluted on about how, when she was at university, Mummy was not the most popular woman around; in fact she was Public Enemy No. 1!

'Clearly used to this backbencher, Mrs Thatcher moved inscrutably on to give a demonstration of dishwashing. This was a misunderstanding of the medium: if you tell a camera a fact the viewer has only limited scope for active disbelief. But put on an unconvincing performance, as here, and we begin to suspect that the cleaning lady has been trussed up in a closet until the telly boys have gone home. But the ordinary people were not voting this time: her party probably realises that if her domestic proclivities become too intolerably demanding she can always run down and do a stint of dishwashing in the House of Commons canteen.'

Appendix III

Average hours spent per week on newspapers and television

	Age			Group	
	15–34	35–54	55 +	AB/C1	C2/DE
Daily/Sunday papers	4·7	6·1	7·4	5·8	6·1
Popular papers	2·8	3·6	4·5	2·8	4·1
Others	1·9	2·5	2·9	3·0	2·1
Television	19·7	18·7	22·6	17·1	22·0
BBC 1	7·1	7·5	9·8	8·6	7·8
BBC 2	1·5	1·4	0·9	1·4	1·2
ITV	11·1	9·8	11·9	7·0	13·0

(*IPC Readership Survey.*)

Appendix IV

Key words used by Heath and Wilson during the February 1974 election campaign

Heath			*Wilson*		
Fair		56	Families		175
Strong		54	families	79	
strong government	12		housewives	33	
law and order	15		British people	63	
firm	17		Crisis and conflict		82
democratic	9		crisis	46	
Moderate		53	divisiveness	23	
moderate	32		confrontation	7	
conciliation	6		conflict	6	
one nation	8		Profiteers and property		
unity	7		speculators		44
Responsible		15	Moderation		21
Militants		15	Fairness		13
Crisis		12	Militants		13
Nationalization		11	Nationalization		11
Parliamentary government		10	nationalization	6	
Conflict (free for all)		9	public ownership	5	
Inflation		8	Fraudulent election		8
British tradition		6	Social contract		7
Social enterprise		5	Socialism		2
The individual		5			

(Analysis of TV election appearances, *New Society*.)

194

Appendix V

Statement by the IBA in June 1974

In April 1974, the new Labour Government extended the life of the Independent Television Authority (as constituted by the IBA Act) from 1976 until 1979, and at the same time similarly extended the contractual life of the BBC, as established by its Charters. In June, the IBA issued a statement of its policy intentions for the period up to 1979.

The main theme of the policy statement is that the system is to remain very much as before, and that another bid for the fourth channel is likely to be forthcoming. The 'diversity' resulting from the regional structure of the ITV network will be maintained, and there is not likely to be an increase in the number of network contractors from the present five. Nor is it envisaged that in 1976 there will be a major re-allocation of the contract areas (for three years only) or an increase in the number of contractors, though some consideration was being given to the policy of sub-dividing regional companies, using local studios. Southern Television, with studios at Southampton and Dover, and HTV, with studios at both Bristol and Cardiff, are cited as examples of how further sub-division is made to work in practice.

In spite of attempts by London Weekend to take television time from Thames, the weekday station, the IBA decided to leave the allocation of transmission hours as it was. It also states that while it feels that the best arrangement is for each region to have only one contractor, applied to London, this policy would mean establishment of a London station that was more than twice the size of any of the other contractors.

The distinction between regional and network companies is to be retained, though the IBA has promised to examine the procedures by which the smaller companies manage to get programmes 'onto the network'. Among the proposals is one that encourages the smaller companies to 'notify the network' (whatever that means) well in advance, before funds are committed to a programme or series, so that the 'network' can decide 'whether and on what terms the programme will find a place in the network schedule.'

Clearly this means that the lot of the smaller companies is scarcely improved, and in practice they would appear to be being discouraged from creating new programmes to offer the network – the decision not to carry on with them possibly being handed to them even at the planning stage. It is to be hoped that the regional companies will

195

largely ignore this procedure and continue to make worthwhile programmes, for which the weight of public opinion will force the network companies to make room.

In view of the short lifespan between 1976 and 1979, the Authority does not intend to invite new applications during 1975, but instead during the latter half of 1974, planned to review the existing companies' progress and make comments and recommendations. In the light of their findings, some restrictions might be applied to the existing franchisees during the period 1976–79.

This last suggestion is little more than a half-hearted attempt by the IBA to be seen to be policing the contracting companies, and it seems unlikely that they will make any better job of it than they have up to 1974. The most we can hope for is firm action by the Government of the day and some constructive recommendations from the new Annan enquiry, announced in the spring of 1974.

Appendix VI

Membership of the Annan Committee on Broadcasting
Lord Annan, Chairman
Tom Jackson, General Secretary, Union of Post Office Workers
Philip Whitehead, Labour MP for Derby North
Sir Marcus Worsley, Conservative MP for Chelsea
Peter Goldman
Professor Hilde Himelweit
Antony Jay
Miss Marghanita Laski
Mrs H. M. Lawrence
A. Dewi Lewis
Sir James MacKay, former Lord Provost of Edinburgh
Mrs Charles Morrison
Dipak Nandy
G. J. Parkes
John D. Pollock
Professor G. D. Sims, Head of Department of Electronics, Southampton University

Bibliography

The Universal Eye, Timothy Green (Bodley Head, 1972). An account of television systems throughout the world.

The Biggest Aspidistra in the World, Peter Black (BBC Publications, 1972). A personal history of the BBC, including radio.

The Least Worst Television in the World, Milton Shulman (Barrie and Jenkins, 1973). An account of the commercial television franchise, which draws on Shulman's experiences as a broadcaster and television critic. Excellent.

The New Priesthood, Joan Bakewell and Nicholas Garnham (Allen Lane, 1970). Comments and interviews with directors, producers, writers on all aspects of television.

The BBC Handbook 1975 (BBC Publications, 1974). Factual account of the previous year's broadcasting and packed with information.

ITV 75: Guide to Independent Television (IBA, 1975). Exactly what it says. Annual survey, plus numerous facts and figures about the IBA and the constituent broadcasting companies. With Radio Supplement.

Broadcasting, Society and the Church (Church Information Office, 1973). Report of the Broadcasting Commission of the General Synod of the Church of England.

The Future of Broadcasting (Eyre Methuen, 1974). The Report to the Social Morality Council.

Television and the People, Brian Groombridge (Penguin, 1972). Covers many aspects of television, including access, information programmes, education, etc.

Children's TV, William Melody (Yale University Press, 1973). Subtitled 'The Economics of Exploitation', looks at children's programming, mainly in America.

The Manufacture of News: Deviance, Social Problems and the Mass Media, Stanley Cohen and Jock Young (Constable, 1973). An assessment of how the news media (including television) handle news coverage of certain issues, such as race, sex, drugs, young people, etc.

Various publications on cable vision can be obtained from the Cable Television Association of Great Britain, 295 Regent Street, London W1. Telephone 01–637 4591.

Index